Praise for
Surrender

T0276577

'Guided by her forthright willingness to examine her own soul and by years of clinical experience, Nicky Clinch teaches self-discovery by means of compassionate, straightforward and powerful practices.'

DR GABOR MATÉ, BESTSELLING AUTHOR OF *IN THE REALM OF HUNGRY GHOSTS*

'This book is the antithesis to the "new you" rhetoric of much of the shallow self-help prevalent today and will show you how, under all that conditioning, your most magnificent self is there waiting.'

ZOE BLASKEY, FOUNDER OF MOTHERKIND

'This powerful, honest book will help you to remember who you truly are and start living in alignment with your soul.'

REBECCA CAMPBELL, BESTSELLING AUTHOR OF *RISE SISTER RISE* AND *THE STARSEED ORACLE*

'Reading this book reminds us of all the ways in which we conform and contort ourselves, and dilute our own urgent truth, and how it is high time we stopped doing so, forever. A battle cry from and for the soul and spirit. Surrender to it.'

EMINÉ RUSHTON, EDITOR OF *OH* MAGAZINE AND CO-AUTHOR OF *SATTVA*

'This powerful book is an important and timely contribution to the collective consciousness at this extraordinary time in our evolution. In order to birth this, first it had to be lived. It was a privilege to witness that process. Nicky laboured and delivered with grace and serenity. Relax, release and surrender. There is no greater message for now.'

EMMA CANNON, MASTER ACUPUNCTURIST, MODERN MEDICINE WOMAN AND AUTHOR

'Authentic, loving, supportive. Nicky speaks straight from her heart to yours. And wht she says is worth listening to.'

BRIGID MOSS, *RED* MAGAZINE

'Nicky Clinch is a force of nature, her work and words are sublime and this book is a gift to humanity. For all those who are ready to let go and step into something bigger, better and brighter, *Surrender* is THE book.'
SUZY ASHWORTH, QUANTUM TRANSFORMATION COACH AND BUSINESS MENTOR

'Nicky Clinch writes as she lives – with courage, clarity and a strong heart. She shares her own journey honestly and openly and invites us all to do the same. *Surrender* is more than a book. It's an invocation of a more real self in a more real world. Nicky's words will touch you deeply.'
YA'ACOV DARLING KHAN, SHAMAN AND BESTSELLING AUTHOR OF
JAGUAR IN THE BODY, BUTTERFLY IN THE HEART AND *SHAMAN*

'Nicky's words and teachings are true medicine for the soul. *Surrender* will help you remember the truth of who you are, who you were born to be and who you have been all along. Get ready to come home.'
MEL WELLS, SPEAKER, COACH AND AUTHOR OF *THE GODDESS REVOLUTION*

'*Surrender* is an empowering deep-dive experience into your own consciousness. Embodying the frequency of surrender, global thought leader Nicky Clinch clearly transmits how you can take back your power so that you can live a life of limitless possibility. Superb!'
REGAN HILLIER, SERIAL ENTREPRENEUR, PHILANTHROPIST, QUANTUM
TRANSFORMATION COACH AND GLOBAL SPEAKER

'This book tells a true story that reveals many deeper truths about the journey all of us are on. It is filled with insight and practical guidance for outgrowing the limits of one's own history, and I recommend it to anyone ready to listen to life as a basis for their further maturation.'
DR DAVID NORRIS, INTERNATIONAL EDUCATOR AND COACH

'In *Surrender*, Nicky shows us a clear roadmap for overcoming obstacles, awakening to our true power and breaking free from our past. A must-read if you are serious about living an inspired life.'
SHANNON KAISER, BESTSELLING AUTHOR OF *THE SELF-LOVE EXPERIMENT*

Surrender

Surrender

Break Free of the Past, Realize Your Power, Live Beyond Your Story

Nicky Clinch

HAY HOUSE

Carlsbad, California • New York City
London • Sydney • New Delhi

Published in the United Kingdom by:
Hay House UK Ltd, The Sixth Floor, Watson House,
54 Baker Street, London W1U 7BU
Tel: +44 (0)20 3927 7290; Fax: +44 (0)20 3927 7291; www.hayhouse.co.uk

Published in the United States of America by:
Hay House Inc., PO Box 5100, Carlsbad, CA 92018-5100
Tel: (1) 760 431 7695 or (800) 654 5126
Fax: (1) 760 431 6948 or (800) 650 5115; www.hayhouse.com

Published in Australia by:
Hay House Australia Pty Ltd, 18/36 Ralph St, Alexandria NSW 2015
Tel: (61) 2 9669 4299; Fax: (61) 2 9669 4144; www.hayhouse.com.au

Published in India by:
Hay House Publishers India, Muskaan Complex,
Plot No.3, B-2, Vasant Kunj, New Delhi 110 070
Tel: (91) 11 4176 1620; Fax: (91) 11 4176 1630; www.hayhouse.co.in

A catalogue record for this book is available from the British Library.

Tradepaper ISBN: 978-1-4019-5985-2
E-book ISBN: 978-1-78817-394-0
Audiobook ISBN: 978-1-78817-604-0

10 9 8 7 6 5 4 3

Interior illustrations: 1, 101, 159 Shutterstock.com/Jag_cz

Printed in the United States of America

*To my children, to whom I owe it
to show this life is truly worth living.*

*To Emma, my anchor and my wings.
Your spirit soars far and wide, my friend.*

To my husband. My soul mate. I love you.

'Surrender is not a weakness.

It is strength.

It takes tremendous strength to

surrender life to the supreme

– to the cosmic unfolding.'

Mooji

Contents

∽ Phase 3: A Birthing ∽

Introduction

'So when you are listening to somebody, completely,
attentively, then you are listening not only to the
words, but also to the feeling of what is being
conveyed, to the whole of it, not part of it.'

JIDDU KRISHNAMURTI

When I'm asked what I do, I explain that I help people grow. 'Grow? Grow into what?' they ask. 'Well, firstly to grow out of who they thought they were, but in essence are not,' I reply. 'Oh,' they say. 'Which allows them to grow into who they were born to be,' I continue. 'But how do you do that?' they ask.

Actually, strictly speaking, I don't do that. What I do is help people clear away what is in the way of their growth – like a butterfly with mud or oil on its wings that prevents it from unfurling them, or a rose bowed down with so much rainwater it cannot reveal its full glory. When you clear away enough of what is blocking and weighing someone down, then growth becomes possible again. And I don't mean the kind of growth through which you get bigger or wider or taller. I mean the kind of growth that is a maturing; a maturing of the body, heart, mind and soul. This is a fundamental part of our nature, to mature and evolve and bloom. I'd even dare to say it is our destiny, as a caterpillar's destiny is to become the butterfly; there are no questions asked, it just is. The destiny of the rose seed is to become the rose; there are no questions asked, it just is. We are no different. Deep within us is a calling, a powerful gravitational pull that draws us home into the fullest, most whole expression of ourselves. In essence, my job is simply to remind you what is already there within you, shining a light on what you have forgotten, so that you can realign once again with who you already are and who you were born on this Earth to become.

This book is my work. The journey of this book is the process I walk people through, as I will do with you. Over the past decade I've been walking people from all parts of life through this maturation process – mothers, fathers, sisters, daughters, brothers – anyone who has a deeper sense that there is much more to this life than just tackling each problem as it arises and just simply continuing to get by. Everyone I've worked with, whether or not they are consciously aware of it initially, has been called to a deeper, more fulfilling relationship with themselves and with life.

And this fulfilment has nothing to do with adding more or finding more or getting more. It becomes possible completely and solely through a process of unlearning, dissolving, releasing and surrendering. Surrendering who we think we are or who we thought we needed to be in order to survive. Surrendering patterns, beliefs and behaviours that do not belong to who we are. Surrendering all of who we are not in order to allow who we are to birth through.

Contrary to what we are taught in our modern world, to surrender is not a weakness. In fact, it takes tremendous strength to let go of what you thought your life should be and surrender yourself to the greater unfolding of what life's dream is for you. It takes tremendous strength to surrender to the cosmic unfolding in order to align with who you were always born to be. It takes tremendous strength to surrender the fight, the control, the masks we wear. We think these are tools to protect ourselves, but in fact they are keeping us more entrenched in our basic survival. It is only through our ability to surrender what we 'know' and our willingness to be catapulted into the complete unknown that we can discover a new possibility for ourselves and for life.

As I write these words, we are in a tremendously challenging time on our planet, and yet I believe this to be a hugely transformational time too. We simply cannot heal what we cannot see, so the first step to any possibility of maturation is to be confronted with all the ways that have not been working, in order to bring them into consciousness. One significant element of the current paradigm – and one that I believe has the possibility of coming to an end – is the conditioning that, for us to be happy, for us to be fulfilled, for us to be free, we must somehow find ways to become bigger, better, tidier, more lovable, more acceptable versions of ourselves, reinforcing the story that who we are right now is not already enough. This is one of the greatest misconceptions of all, and is part of what must now come to a completion. Because this way of being on our planet and in our lives comes from a place of separation and 'not enough', which has led us to live led by this separation and creating more separation in our world. Our internal suffering as individual human beings is not separate from the suffering and struggles occurring on our planet today.

The way in which we have been living is connected to the wellbeing of our planet – and thus our healing is our planet's healing.

The calling for us to remember who we truly are is getting greater by the day, in order for us to live from our wholeness, not from the separation.

This book is for every single one of you who no longer wishes to participate in this misconception, which has disempowered you and kept you blocked from knowing your true power and your full, whole, authentic selves. This book is for every one of you who is no longer prepared to consider it an option to carry on living a life that someone else told you was the one you should be living, instead of living a life aligned with who you really are. This book will help you begin asking fundamental questions in order to live into the discovery of the answers:

- Why am I here?

- Is how I'm living serving me?

- How can I love more than I love now?

- Is how I'm living serving life itself?

- Am I free?

If you are now ready to surrender simply surviving your life to the service of discovering what it means to be fully alive, in alignment with who you were born to be, then it is not an accident that you've picked up this book at this time. Surrender is a spiritual path: the more we clear the way, the more of what is true can emerge. It's like mining for diamonds; we dust away layers and layers of earth, wondering if anything is changing at all, when all of a sudden we uncover a diamond that had been there all along. Surrender is a love story in which you learn that it is possible to heal fully and to know your wholeness. It's a love story with yourself, as it is your own love that will heal you. Surrender is a way of being in life where you become the dance and life is the dancer. And you remember who you are and thus remember your connection to life itself.

So welcome, I'm tremendously happy that you are here. I've been waiting for you.

My Story

Twenty years ago my life hit rock-bottom. It was my first moment of true surrender, and it burst open the gateway to my maturation. By the age of 20, I'd already spent nearly a decade lost in a haze of drugs, alcohol, bulimia, men, self-hate and self-abandonment. Those final days are etched forever into my memory. In the mornings, when I woke, I'd have a few blissful moments of reprieve, when my mind would be still and I hadn't yet remembered how I was living; micro-moments that allowed me to feel as though I was breathing before the tidal wave of my reality would smash down and drown me again with a torrent of abuse: *I'm such a failure. I'm so disgusting. I hate myself. I'm a completely worthless person.* Followed quickly by a frantic attempt to try and fix my life and change: *Today I'm going to stay clean and detox and eat only salad and I won't purge. Today I'm going to change my life and it'll all be good.* Every day I'd get out of bed filled with hope that this would be the day when everything would be different, but sadly it never was. It was like being stuck on a hamster wheel trying to find a way off – each time I tried to move forwards, I ended up back in the same place as before. It was a devastating existence. And it wasn't the drugs or the alcohol or the purging that hurt so much; it was how worthless and hopeless I was feeling inside, thus leaving me in a constant state of disconnection – from myself and from something greater.

The day I hit rock-bottom, I got out of bed with the usual false hope. Suddenly I felt as though I'd been hit by a ton of bricks, and I collapsed to the floor. I broke down completely and, there on the floor of my living room, I cried tears I'd been holding in forever. It was as though my heart had finally smashed into a million pieces and I was no longer trying to stop it. Through my emotion, I began to experience something I'd never experienced before. A wave of peacefulness – a stillness, a spaciousness – moved through me and left everything quiet within me. I swear with all my heart it was as though God or Source, or something that felt like pure love, came to sit right next to me. Before I knew it, I'd whispered these words:

'I want to live but I don't know how; I surrender.'

I didn't consciously know it at the time, but that was the moment I began to let go of everything I'd been trying so desperately to cling on to – the point at which I completely surrendered. In that moment I was ready either to die or to learn how to live. Before I knew it, I found myself in a doctor's office, sharing the whole truth of all that I'd been hiding from everyone and even myself. Within a matter of days, I had entered treatment for my addiction, I had a therapist, and I had embarked on what I now know to be the most remarkable healing journey – a journey that has continued to evolve and grow and bloom during the course of the past two decades. Surrendering that day was both the end and also the beginning – of everything I had ever known about who I thought I was, and about discovering who I truly am. Yes, I've struggled; and yes, I've fallen flat on my face many times; and no, it hasn't been all smooth sailing. Life will always be life, messy, ever-changing, moving – sometimes up, sometimes down. But my relationship with life and with myself has been led by, and committed to, the process that we will walk together through the pages of this book. At each threshold of growth and healing for me, I've had to make the conscious decision to surrender, again and again and again; each time dissolving more of what is in the way; each time allowing more of who I truly am to birth through.

My maturation has not been about finding myself or about becoming a bigger, better version of myself. Instead, it has been a birthing of myself; an emerging of the version of me I'd been searching for – a version that had been within me all along. Discovering how to hear my own heart, my own voice, my own inner wisdom, which had been buried beneath the incessant noise of my mind. Learning to listen from this place of discovery has taught me to trust myself and to trust life. It has taught me that I have always been enough.

Nowadays my life feels like an intimate dance between life and myself, without really knowing what the next steps are going to be. In order for us to truly be able to dance together, I have to stay awake and open to hearing the music. Neither one of us is leading the other; we are in a complete co-creation state of being. To continue to be in this majestic dance, I need to continue to live beyond the noise of my mind and beyond the stories and fears and programming that block the flow. While I no longer have much need to live in the past, it has been very necessary to continue to look at what I carry from there. I have had to live and breathe every moment – the good and the bad, the shadow and the light, the rough and the smooth – in order for me to integrate it as my own embodied truth. Coming out on the other side of this process, I've felt destined to pass on what I've learned to the many of you that are being called, as I was.

During the course of the past two decades, I've trained and qualified in aspects of Traditional Chinese Medicine (TCM), learning about illness and imbalance and health. I've studied and researched the impact that unhealed trauma has on how we know ourselves and see ourselves in the world. I've learned how this leads us to latch on to defence mechanisms and masks, behavioural patterns and beliefs, in order to protect ourselves from pain. I've trained and continue to train in maturation facilitation and leadership, studying the nature and culture of human beings, the power and impact of the mind, and how the stories we identify with can contaminate our reality. I've apprenticed myself to shamans in the Amazon, working intensely with the indigenous wisdom of plant medicines. But by far my greatest training and teacher has been life itself. Everything I teach I've lived. I was once taught that life can be either a torture chamber or the greatest education there is, and I've chosen to commit to making life the school in which I'm a perpetual student.

You may be as deep as I was in that struggle on the hamster wheel, or maybe you are just touching in and out. Either way, I want you to know that I understand what it feels like to be in that pain and to want so much to become free. If you're like I was, you may be wondering whether you should give up on the whole thing altogether, or whether the whispers of the dreams that lie within your heart could ever become possible. Know that it is not only possible for you to become free of the struggle, but that your dreams are waiting for you to do so, so that you can live them, so that you can fulfil them, and so that you can allow life to express itself through you while doing so. That is why I've written this book for you, and I'm so thankful that you have been able to trust enough in something to pick up this book and to begin reading it at this particular time in your life. I want to invite you to entertain the possibility that this is not by accident, but exactly as it is meant to be. You may now be ready to surrender what you know of yourself, how you were 'meant' to be living, and who you thought you were meant to be, in order to grow, mature and birth into who you were *born* to be.

How to Use the Book

Within the pages of this book I'm going to walk you through a process of maturation. I'm going to teach you this by placing words of truth on these pages and leading you through a process that could create real, lasting transformation in how you are living your life and who you are being in it. But, in order for this to happen, you cannot just read the words, conceptualize them, understand them and then simply adopt them as your own truth purely because I said so. Because this will change literally nothing for you.

Instead, I invite you to take these teachings, take this truth, and allow them in. Allow them to affect you and integrate them into your life to begin living them yourself. Only through your own direct experience of living and exploring these teachings will they transform from information I've shared with you into real, embodied knowledge and into your own truth. It is only through your own embodied truth and understanding that your maturation can occur, because you are the source and power of all that you may have been seeking up to now. Throughout this process, you are going to discover just how courageous and powerful you really are, and that everything you have been looking for is within you already.

The three phases of this book I've chosen and named very deliberately, as they represent, capture and express exactly what it feels like to experience each phase. Within each chapter there are many inquiries, practices, meditations and exercises that I invite you to participate in. Please do allow yourself to do them, as these are the parts of the book that will show you how to integrate the learnings directly into your own lives. These are the parts in which the shifts and change will really occur. I also share clients' stories in which names and specific details have been changed to protect individuals' privacy, but the human experiences, insights and points of maturation are all accurate.

Phase 1: An Ending

This phase looks at the areas of your life and who you have been in it that are not working, have not been serving you, and have been blocking your growth. Every moment of awareness and insight you experience offers you the possibility of – and invitation to – surrender. Through this process you'll be gaining awareness of the stories from your past that have been contaminating your present, dissolving those blocks and the power they have had over you and your life. By surrendering that which is not aligned with who you truly are, you create openings for new possibilities to emerge.

Phase 2: Love

In this phase you will learn to love again, by ingraining new behaviours, showing up, and adopting new practices and patterns that come from listening and honouring what is authentic and true to who you genuinely are. In the very act of dissolving your old patterns and thinking you can create a new foundation based on love and worth and authenticity and truth.

Phase 3: A Birthing

This phase teaches you how to dance with life led from the present moment, connecting deeply with who you truly are, building trust and truth and wisdom and power. It will align you with life's dream for you and help you become a co-creator in the unfolding of your life and who you were born to be.

The process of this book is a spiritual path that will connect you deeper to Source and to life itself, but it is also a way of being embodied as a human being in life, allowing a new sense of freedom and aliveness and purpose and meaning to every part of how you live it. And finally, this process is a love story. One in which you rediscover a love for yourself, learning to *be* love rather than seek it. Discovering that it is in fact your own love that will be what heals you. Because you do deserve to heal – in fact, it is your destiny to heal, to know your true authentic wholeness. It is your destiny to come home.

So ignite your heart, summon your courage and strap yourself in for the journey.

Here we go.

Nicky x

Self-commitment Declaration

Contrary to what you might feel you know about yourself, you are actually the one who has all the power. Therefore you need to be the one who makes the choice and the commitment of your heart and soul to your healing and maturation.

So my first question to you, which I invite you to let in deeply within yourself, is: are you ready now to do whatever it takes in order to be free?

If the answer within you is YES, congratulations. This will be your anchor throughout this whole process and onwards. And so, just for the sake of power and intention, let's get this down in writing.

A teacher once taught me that our writing is the expression of our heart truths that flow straight from our heart, right down our arm, onto the page. Therefore, what we write is our heart speaking.

Please pledge your commitment TO YOURSELF here:

I, ...[*write your name here*], am now willing to do what it takes to surrender fully to the process, in service and honour to my healing and to becoming free.

I, ...[*write your name here*], hereby make a full and heartfelt commitment to myself and to my life: from this point forwards, and throughout the process of this book, and throughout my life thereafter, I'm ready and willing to show up 100 per cent for myself, for my authenticity, and for the process of my unfurling into alignment; and I'm ready to face and feel all that needs to be faced and felt, as an act of love and honouring for myself and my heart. I won't abandon myself by abandoning the process.

I will not punish myself for doing this imperfectly.

I will be gentle and go easy on myself as I allow myself to heal.

I will always allow myself to bring compassion and love to all the parts I find challenging.

I will honour myself and my courage for being here and doing this work.

I will keep going to the end of the book no matter how long it takes.

I, ... [*write your name here*], hereby make the conscious decision to SURRENDER to the process, even if I do not fully understand it, and as I dive deeper into the unknown.

I ....[*write your name here*], am hereby resolved that I'm no longer willing to stay stuck nor to continue merely surviving as I have been in the past. I'm ready to live in pure alignment with my true authentic self.

....

[*add your signature here*]

PHASE 1

An Ending

Endings are never really endings;

they are beginnings in disguise.

～

CHAPTER 1

The Beginning of the End

*'Until you make the unconscious conscious, it
will direct your life and you will call it fate.'*

CARL JUNG

There is a consistent thread that runs through the experience of almost every person who finds themselves coming to me to work together. Each one of them is faced with some form of a breakdown in their lives, whether due to their health, emotional or mental wellbeing, professional situation, or all of the above. And it is extremely distressing for them, because something that once worked – ways of being in their lives that they had been able to rely on to get them through – had become shaky, fragile, unreliable, even broken. Creating so much pain; so much fear, panic and hopelessness.

The natural human instinct is to try as hard as possible to scramble our way back – to fix it, save it, change it – anything to get back to how things were and to what we know.

But what if we were to lean *into* the breaking rather than away from it? What if the breaking is exactly what needs to happen, or what is meant to happen? What if we simply cannot truly heal, evolve, transform in any form without this breaking first?

What if the only way forwards is to surrender completely into the breakdown?

From Breakdown to Breakthrough

Almost every spiritual teaching on the journey of awakening speaks about this important and necessary phase: the dissolving – the destruction of what we once thought we knew to be true about who we are and what our life is – in order to allow something new, more authentic and more true to emerge and evolve through.

When I see clients facing this point in their journey, as distressing as it is for them, I know that it shows that they are now ready to heal on a much deeper level. I know they are ready to embark on a process of coming home to a more authentic version of themselves. I see it almost as a sign from Source, like a loving nudge on the shoulder saying, 'Now is the time for more healing, my dear.'

But goodness, it takes remarkable courage to embrace the breakdown in this way. Facing something head-on that we know is likely to prove painful for us. Leaning in to something that is leading us into the complete unknown, like rowing across an ocean towards unknown lands without any real guarantee we will not fall off the ends of the Earth. My God, this takes courage, and I'm forever humbled and inspired by every single being that embarks on this journey.

I'm going to assume that this is why you are here with me now: because something is beginning to or has already broken down in your life. Maybe your body is not feeling so healthy or working like it used to, or the relationships you find yourself in are bringing up endless pain for you, or the job you're working in keeps filling you with the same dread and dissatisfaction. Maybe you're finding yourself in constant emotional turmoil and you just can't bear it any longer, or your levels of fear and panic and obsession are taking over your life. Maybe you're struggling with anger that never seems to go away, or drinking or drug-taking that no longer seems to give you a reprieve. Whatever it is – a pattern or habit or perception of who you are or how your life is coming to an end – it feels as though in some form or other it is the end of your world.

So, the first thing I want to ask you to do, right now in this moment, is to try to breathe a little deeper. Please take a moment to close your eyes, bring forth the part of your life or yourself that feels as though it is breaking down, and become aware of the feelings that are there. For now, without knowing what you're going to do about it or how you're going to fix it or change it, I ask you to simply notice the feeling in your body and take a few really deep slow breaths in, with long slow exhalations out. For now, allow yourself to just breathe nice and deeply into your body without needing to know any more than that. Continue breathing deeply like this for a few more moments and then, when you are ready, open your eyes.

Instead of fighting or resisting this breakdown I want to invite you to surrender to it. Allow the vulnerability to come with compassion and tenderness. And remember that choice I mentioned earlier, about deciding to trust. Because if you can find the courage to move away from the hardening and the fighting and the grasping, and instead lean in to softening, you can allow this momentum to lead you through the unknown towards the home of your heart and truth. Because the other way to interpret a breakdown is as a break*through*. The other way to view a challenge is as an opportunity.

I'm going to invite the possibility that, right here, right now, like my courageous clients, you too have received a nudge from Source that it is now your time for a much deeper form of healing and your time to come home to a more authentic version of you.

My Breakthrough

A few months before starting the process of writing this book, I returned to the Amazon jungle in Peru to participate in a two-week transformational alignment retreat working with plant medicines. It was my second trip to the Amazon over a 10-year period.

Three days into the process, something very uncomfortable began niggling at me.

My husband and I had not been in a good place for a long time. In our nine years together, we just kept revisiting the same problems over and over again. Whenever I'd come to him with anything I needed to communicate – maybe something I was struggling with or something I needed help with – it would end up with him feeling controlled, managed and criticized by me. And so my need for him to hear me, see me and show up for me emotionally would end up with him feeling trapped, leading him to withdraw and pull away – literally the exact opposite of what I needed. The pain that would result from this dynamic was excruciating for me and I know it was extremely painful for him too. I'd feel so abandoned, so let down, so disappointed, so alone. After many years of this same fight happening over and over again, the deep-seated disappointment and hurt within me reached peak levels. In my heart I'd begun to give up on ever believing he was someone I could trust or lean on, so I threw myself into my work and started living my life as if he wasn't really part of it. By the time I left for Peru, we were living under the same roof and parenting our children together, but that was as far as our partnership went.

It was so painful but I had no idea what to do about it and, to be honest, I was terrified to change it. There was just so much to lose. We had a whole life together with two very young children, so I just pushed it away and focused on aligning every other area of my life, resigning myself to accept that this was just the way it was going to be.

But once I was in the jungle it became completely impossible to ignore any longer.

On the very first day, I learned that for us to be truly in alignment in our life, it can't just apply to *some* of our life but must encompass *all* of our life.

So I began looking at how I behaved in work, with my children, with the customer-service guy on the phone, with myself and in my marriage. True alignment is *everything* about who I am and what I stand for in my life. So as I got brutally honest with myself about my life, I immediately began feeling like a complete fraud. My life had become almost entirely aligned with my calling, teaching and leading others to live aligned with their authentic empowered selves. But my behaviour within my marriage, and the person I was being in it, was the complete opposite. That moment of realization hit like a hard kick in the stomach, as only the real deep truth emerging from a place of total denial can feel.

As the retreat went on, I began to see how much I was neglecting myself by living in this dynamic with my husband. How much I was failing to care for my own needs, not being my true authentic self, and suppressing my feelings and my voice. I saw clearly that I had so completely given up on ever feeling as though my needs could be met that I had stopped even trying or even caring any more. And as long as I continued to do this I was completely abandoning myself and my truth, which went completely against what I had committed to my life being about.

This behaviour echoed exactly how I'd felt as a child. Having my emotional and deeper needs met as a child just wasn't possible, so I'd resigned myself to not even trying or caring.

It was devastating for me to see so clearly how I was re-enacting my childhood within this marriage. And it brought up a world of sadness and grief for me.

But also deep, deep healing. I needed to face this breakdown in my life full-on, otherwise I'd never have any opportunity to heal it.

As I came to the end of the retreat, I knew I was worthy of having my needs met and I was ready to let go of this pattern of giving up on myself. I was fully committed to living in a different way and to creating a life in which I too would allow myself to have my needs fully met. I was ready to make an uncompromising stand for my own healing and truth.

As I prepared to return home, I had no idea what was going to happen in my marriage but I knew I was no longer willing to live as before. Something fundamental was going to have to change.

Healing, Not Fixing

We live in a world obsessed with fixing things, but there is a big difference between 'fixing' and 'healing'. Fixing is looking at the thing that is broken and trying to put it back together the way it was before. With fixing no change occurs; no new possibility, no growth, no expansion. Merely finding the way back to where you were.

Healing is a whole other process. Healing is looking at what is broken and using the opportunity to dive into a deeper process of discovering what might be causing the 'breaking'; diving deeply into an exploration of what hasn't been working in order to learn from it. And then releasing the elements that contributed to the breaking and adopting new elements that will work much better. In the healing process we evolve, grow, expand into a new way of being. That breaking allows an evolution to occur, and through it we can allow something much more positive to emerge.

There is a distinct possibility that those areas of your life that are causing you the most pain are not actually the problem. They may be occurring and showing up and repeating themselves over and over again for a reason. They do not need fixing; they are the entry points through which you can experience your deepest levels of healing. They are the gateways to your growth and expansion. They are showing you where to look. They are calling you to look into them, so that you can come home to your wholeness, so that you can heal. This may be a lot to get your head around, so let me tell you a story.

Sally's Story

When Sally came to me for help, she suffered from many major health issues: extreme allergies (even to dust), low energy, swollen eyes, painful digestion, constant mucus, skin breakouts and heart palpitations. She had seen every doctor under the sun and had been on steroids and antihistamines for years, which had made her feel worse and caused her to become distraught. Emotionally and mentally, she was in a constant state of anxiety, panic and fear, and had lost all confidence in herself and in her life. She was clearly going through a breakdown.

When I looked at Sally, her whole body, energy and emotional state seemed to be paralysed in complete panic. The kind of frozen shock caused by unresolved childhood trauma. I immediately began working with her to draw out the information that would reveal where this shock might have come from. And, as it turned out, a close family member had died suddenly when she was very young, and she had never done any healing work around it.

This was what I was looking for. The doorway in. All her 'problems' were leading back to the same place: her physical health issues, allergies, skin breakouts, mucus. In TCM all these symptoms are connected to the lungs, and on an emotional level TCM connects the lungs with grief. Her anxiety and panic; her sense of being let down by life and let down by the medical system; her feeling there was no way out and everything was falling apart: all of these emotions mirrored the experience she had had when she discovered her father had died.

A moment in time, a trauma, that had caused her to freeze and disconnect from her authentic self. A moment that had never been healed and, as a result, was repeating itself over and over again in her adult life.

In our first session together, I took her straight to that moment in time through a regression process I use. That moment when a little girl woke up one morning to find the whole world as she had known it broken. As I led her gently into that moment in time, I invited her to be fully with whatever she experienced without running away or resisting. Her memory of that day was of numbness. She never cried a single tear; she just numbed out. Buried beneath the numbness, however, her heart had shattered, and subconsciously she had resolved to freeze within herself and never to trust life again. In the session, Sally's frozen state began to thaw as she broke down in deep, sobbing grief. She surrendered all her fight and resistance as the emotion moved through her like a dam of energy flowing once more. The frozen wall around her heart began to thaw and her heart opened once again.

It was a breakthrough that allowed the rest of her transformation to unfold from a completely new space.

The story Sally had completely identified with – 'I can never trust life again' – had been contaminating her whole life, leading her to live in a state of constant avoidance, escape and victimhood. Always presuming that something terrible was coming around the corner. The process Sally and I worked through is the process I'll lead you through in this book. A process of surrendering in order to allow the true, authentic self to emerge.

Sally is now almost entirely symptom-free. She enrolled back in school, qualified as a herbalist and will go on to help many others with their own healing. Without a doubt, Sally is experiencing her life in a remarkable new way – a way of being that was already within her and that becomes more and more available to her as she continues to surrender all that is not authentic to her. And the fundamental point to this story is that her route home to her authentic self *only* became available when she turned her gaze inwards to look at the loud callings of her 'problems' and breakdown. They were the gateways to her path home.

Your breakdown is not the problem. It is the gateway to your breakthrough.

EXERCISE: GETTING STARTED

So let's start at the beginning. Get your journal out and write as much as you need around the following questions:

1. Why are you here? Why did you pick up this book? If you were to get super-honest with yourself, what is beginning to break down in your life? What is no longer working for you? What are the details? How does it feel? How have you been trying to avoid it, stop it, resist it? How has that affected you? Get your heart out on the page as you begin with where you are right now.

2. Are you willing to admit now that running from it and resisting it has not been working for you?

3. Are you ready to now face it, to look into it rather than turning away, and to be open to the possibility that your breakthrough is on the other side of the breakdown?

4. What insights, 'aha!' moments or sprinkles of possibility come to you from reading the chapter above? Write these down as your points of light.

Answering the Call

Humans are often searching for the bridge to get to the other side of the river. They hope and believe that on the other side they'll find everything that is good, everything that is whole, everything that will fulfil and complete them. If only they can get 'there'. The 'happy ending'.

But there is not and never has been a bridge, nor another side, nor a happy ending.

All there is is you, and life, and here and now.

When I share this with my clients, there is almost always the same response: a sense of loss and a sense of peace in exactly the same moment. But mostly a sense of loss.

What comes up for you as I tell you this? Take a moment to connect with what occurs for you as you read this news: that there is no magic bridge you can find that will get you to the magical place where everything will be good?

Is there a feeling of loss? Maybe even anger, irritation, frustration?

I remember the very first time I heard it, about nine years ago. I was in the middle of a maturation programme myself, and I felt the most enormous surge of rage well up within me. Within seconds I stood up and started challenging the facilitator; I remember wanting to throw my chair at her I felt so angry. In that moment she was taking away the one thing I'd been holding on to so tightly: that if I could just find that bridge I'd be okay.

There had to be a 'there'. There had to be a 'happy ending', and I needed to find the 'thing' that would get me there so I could finally be 'happy'.

Without it… what's left?

Loss. The loss of that hope; the loss of the fairy tale in which there is a guaranteed happy ending.

Feeling this loss is completely understandable and I invite you to allow yourself to give it much room if it's there for you. Because the death of a fantasy – one that feeds and drives so many of us through our lives – is extremely painful. But that fantasy keeps us in a place of hoping: hoping that one day it will all be better: that one day, someday, somewhere out there, it will be better and all our problems will disappear.

This hope keeps us in a constant state of illusion, keeping our focus perpetually on the future, on somewhere that doesn't exist. It prevents us from truly or fully allowing or welcoming what 'is' in the present moment of *now*. We are stuck in a state of fantasy rather than truly *being* present and connected at home in ourselves.

The feeling of loss doesn't surprise me, but what does surprise me is the feeling of peace that can often come too. A relief of some sort. Somehow, somewhere deep within us all, we don't really want to have to be searching so hard: the constant searching and seeking is such an exhausting way to live. Somewhere deep within us, consciously or subconsciously, we all want to be able to let go of the search and simply *be* at home, in ourselves and in the present moments of now.

We all long to simply *be*.

Finding Our Truth

Every single one of us, without exception, arrives on this Earth whole and complete. We all emerge in a deep state of connection, being in the present moment, with Source, with life and with love.

When my son Calum was born, I observed him so closely, so intently, and I learned so much from him. In his newborn state, he was completely connected to the now in every moment. For him there was no past, there was no future, there was just the present moment. I learned that, during his first few weeks, he did not yet distinguish himself and me as separate beings. There was no 'me' or 'you' yet in his world. We were completely connected, united; we were one. Everything around him was an extension of himself and me and everything all at once.

This is why it is so magical to spend time with children: because it keeps us wholly in the present moment, and I believe it awakens something within us that remembers this is who we too once were. And this is who we authentically are.

All the things that we think are 'wrong with us' are actually survival strategies developed as our response to trauma or pain in early childhood. Our patterns, behaviours, beliefs – they are not who we are. They have been inherited, passed on to us from others, learned and programmed.

But that is not who we are.

Deep within each one of us there is a profound longing for truth and for peace. We yearn to return to a space of belonging, of home.

Our authentic state of being, in which we can simply *be*.

It is if we are living in a deep state of homesickness, without knowing that is what it is.

As Ram Dass said, 'We're all just walking each other home.'

Following this longing is like following something that we cannot see but somehow choose to trust is there, consciously or subconsciously. With the intention to come to a place of truth rather than simply to feel better. To come to a place of authenticity.

Eckhart Tolle wrote that it is our human destiny to come home to our truth – to that place beyond our mind, beyond our programming. To our authentic aligned self.

Like a swarm of monarch butterflies that somehow manages to navigate its death-defying way across thousands of miles to come home to the same patch of forest in Mexico every single year, we must answer the

Every one of us arrives on this Earth
whole and complete, with a deep
connection to the present moment,
to Source, to life and to love.

This is who you are.

Remember.

~

call home to our human destiny too. When we honour it and commit to it we are supported by life all the way.

Gina's Story

Gina signed up to work with me on her relationship with her job in the finance sector. It didn't align with her heart: she felt she needed the financial security, but it left her drained and exhausted, with no room in her life for anything that brought her joy, which was her creativity.

Gina struggled greatly with disassociation. She'd disconnect from allowing herself to experience any feelings and disengage from her whole body. She lived in a constant state of fear, leading her to shut down, unable to express her true self. Often she felt alone and detached from herself, from others and from life.

When we first met, all she could see before her were the barriers to change; certain that things were just the way they were, and she simply had to deal with it.

Yet there was something else within her that she didn't understand, something that kept whispering about how there might be another way. I invited her to trust this unknown something within her and to surrender to the process that unfolded.

Two weeks later, something remarkable happened.

She found out a close family member had become very unwell and, just like that, her entire life as she'd known it was turned upside down. When she called to tell me, I knew: this was life intervening, and something much, much bigger was unfolding that neither she nor I could yet understand.

When Gina was three years old, she'd become extremely sick and nearly died. The trauma of that experience, frozen within her, led her to identify with the story that life was dangerous. Thus she lived in fear and sought always to be in control, disassociating from anything that felt 'uncontrollable', such as feelings, creativity, intimacy – everything that represented truly living.

In this moment, when their lives were being turned upside down, there was an invitation to heal deeply, to surrender what was inauthentic and out of alignment. This was part of her maturation and her commitment to answering the call home.

Within weeks, she'd been given compassionate leave on full pay, and suddenly she had time, plus financial security.

Every bit of the rigid control she'd formerly exerted over her life crumbled and she was forced to surrender to the complete unknown. In her surrender she began to feel again. All the fear, grief and sadness that she'd kept buried within for her whole life, she now felt ready to fully face up to. Everything unfolding in her life was inviting her to show up in a completely new way. One in which she had to surrender and simply be present with each step, in each day, not knowing what was going to unfold next. She made the decision to trust in a much bigger process, even if she couldn't see how it would turn out.

In a session I led her back to the frozen moment of trauma when she was a sick child. Here she realized she hadn't known how to express what she was feeling to her parents, so instead she'd just given up and shut down – a pattern she could see had been repeating over and over throughout her life in almost every single area. In the process, she surrendered all resistance and became fully present to the powerlessness she'd experienced as that little girl; and also to how she still managed to break through and get better. As the frozen shock of that trauma began to dissolve within her, Gina began to soften and relax. She was able to see how even with no control she still made it through, and her relationship with life and who she is in it began to shift.

This softening and surrender was able to support her throughout the whole process with her partner and allowed her to share her feelings more, ask for help, and support and trust to the bigger process.

As we came to the end of the year, her family member had thankfully recovered from their illness. What a remarkable outcome. And Gina could see how everything had unfolded exactly as it should. The moment she made that contract with life to answer her calling home, she surrendered to such a deep process of healing and alignment. Just as you did at the beginning of this book.

Today she has a trust in life that's so deep it runs through everything she does and how she lives. She completed her qualifications and is helping many people just like herself. All while allowing herself to experience more joy, beauty and peace. No matter what, Gina kept answering the call for her. It may not have unfolded in the way she wanted, but it was absolutely the way she needed. Her job was to surrender and commit to each step of the way.

As it is for you.

There is no bridge. There is no other side. There is only you and here and now and your intention. And that is already enough.

Answering Your Call

If we can be courageous enough to let go of the fantasy, to let go of the searching, and to face what is already within us, we allow something to emerge that is much more remarkable, sacred, aligned and authentic.

This can only be possible if we are willing to surrender to what is and continuously choose to commit to answering the call.

And so let's go back together a few pages: remember at the beginning when I invited you to consider the possibility that you picking up this book at this particular time in your life was not an accident? And that it is likely to be because now is your time? Well, it is. You are here because something within you is calling you to answer your calling home too. So trust the process and know that when following this you will be supported.

EXERCISE: YOUR VISION

I'd like to invite you to get your journal out and complete the following exercise.

1. Firstly, visualize 24 hours of your ideal day as you envision it. Describe this vision for your life and how you wish to experience yourself being you in it. Write it in as much detail as you can, focusing mostly on how you are feeling and experiencing yourself being you in the vision. For example: *I wake up in the morning and I feel peace and contentment and restful freedom. I'm lying next to my partner and there is a heartfelt connection between us. My children jump into bed and we laugh and play and hug each other.* Keep writing until you have described an entire day in the life of being you in this vision.

2. Once you've written it, read your vision out loud, allowing yourself to read it slowly and consciously. Let yourself experience each moment you're describing in your whole body as if it's real. If you can, find someone you trust and feel safe with and read the vision out to them too, so it's shared with another.

3. Put it up somewhere so that you can see it every single day.

4. Write down one or two moments in your life when remarkable, unexplained things happened in which you were completely and fully supported by life, even though your fears told you that you wouldn't be.

'PRESENCE AND FELT-SENSE' MEDITATION

Sit comfortably and close your eyes. Take a deep, slow, conscious breath in, allowing it to enter your body at a soft, tender pace, creating a spaciousness within you, slowing you right down.

As you exhale, simply let the breath release and then repeat that slow inhalation, creating more space, slowing you down to meet yourself here in the present.

Continue to breathe in this way but do not push; do not try too hard. Simply let your body breathe itself, as you bring your awareness inwards to meet yourself.

Notice what is present: any emotions, any tension, anything – sadness, anger, self-consciousness, fear, doubt, irritation…. Whatever it is, simply notice it without judgement; without trying to change it or fix it. Just observe and then acknowledge it, with your mind's eye describing what you see.

Observe any feelings moving through you, simply observing and being with them, as you return to meeting yourself and all the life that moves through you, in the present.

When you have finished, simply allow your breathing to regulate into a normal rhythm and slowly open your eyes.

Write in your journal anything you saw, noticed or learned.

Continue sitting and breathing and meeting yourself in this way for 10 minutes each day.

Solving Problems from the Source of the Problems Creates Problems

Amy came to work with me a few years back. From the outside, it would have been easy to look at her and wonder if there was anything she was struggling with at all. She ran an extremely successful business, was in good health, had vibrant energy, had the big house and the loving husband. From the viewpoint of the world we live in, she ticked the box of 'having it all'.

Yet inside she felt empty and lost.

Her words to me were: 'Nicky, I did it all "perfectly". I got the house, the marriage, the money, the job, the body. And yet I feel so unhappy. Why?'

The way Amy felt is such a common phenomenon for many in our modern world. We're so convinced that if we just do the right things – look the right way, achieve a certain level of success, drink the right green juice, eat the perfect foods, or get the followers on social media – then we may just be able to know our own value and worth. But trying to fix our sense of emptiness and unworthiness by turning to solutions 'out there' is never going to give us what we truly want and need; it simply reaffirms that the feelings of emptiness and unworthiness were already within us from the start.

We can never have enough of what we never really wanted in the first place.

In our attempts to fix our problems we latch on to what we can 'out there' in the hope it will make us 'feel better'. As if 'feeling better' is the ultimate solution to all our problems. We drink the green juice, we do the workshop, we get the partner or the house and we may feel 'better' for a while. But after a while – often only a short while – those old familiar problems start creeping back. Maybe we feel inadequate or unimportant, anxious that life is not safe, or invisible and insignificant; maybe it manifests as recurring feelings of dread and anxiety within us, or we find ourselves revisiting old obsessions and worries – whatever it is, it's likely we've been here before. And in our disappointment we tell ourselves that that man wasn't the right one, or that job, or that juice, and our quest to 'feel better' continues as we search for the next solution 'out there' in the hope that next time it'll finally work.

Even describing this is so painful, because it is such an empty cycle that leads nowhere. And sadly most of humanity is stuck in this cycle today. In our quest to 'fix' the problem 'out there' we're not really seeing what the true solution is: to know that who we are, as we are, is already enough.

Amy and I worked together to identify the root of the story she was stuck in: the constant striving for external perfection – calorie-counting, endless hours in the gym; the push for more and more success and affirmation in her work; how she was never able to be present in the here and now. She saw how, after many years of living this way, the 'high' she used to get from her successes and from getting things perfect just didn't happen any more. Instead, the more she strived, the more empty and lost she felt, as if stuck on a hamster wheel with no idea how to get off.

What was it then that Amy really wanted, do you think?

It had nothing to do with the external image she was trying so hard to project. In fact, the more she tried to find an external solution to her problems, the more problems she created within herself.

Do you identify with Amy? Cast your awareness over your life. In the quest to try to solve your problems and feel better, have you ended up creating more problems within yourself? I invite you to be completely non-judgemental here as you allow yourself to see this clearly.

We cannot heal what we cannot see first.

In latching onto something 'out there', in the hope it'll finally allow us to feel whole, we're rejecting, judging and resisting the person we are now and the life experiences that are rising within us in the present – creating more suffering as we try to solve an internal problem with an external solution.

By trying to solve the problem from the source of the problem, we validate and deepen the problem: the place of lack within us.

Here's a question: if you knew you were already whole and enough within yourself, would there be any need to prove yourself, strive and push, grasp and control or compensate for anything? Take a moment to reflect. The true answer is no. When you're living from a place of wholeness there's nothing to prove. But trying to compensate for internal lack with external validation will just make you feel more empty inside, getting you stuck in a cycle of self-rejection, pain and suffering.

There will never be enough clothes, food, drink, or money, when all you really wanted was whole and complete love.

Amy identified that, for as long as she could remember, she'd had a deep-seated belief that she was not 'enough' as she was. As a result, she'd felt driven to improve herself through her appearance and professional success. As a little girl, Amy had been aware that her father worked all the time. He'd leave for work before she woke in the morning and get back from work after she had gone to bed. Even at the weekends he'd lock himself away in his office working for hours in a whirlwind of stress and distraction. At the time, she told herself that his lack of availability must be because she wasn't enough in herself. Maybe if she was better – more beautiful, more bright, more *anything* – then he would drop everything to show her the attention she longed for from him. And so her quest for being better began.

In her healing, Amy began to learn how to be with her feeling of 'not enough' and her sense of unworthiness. Instead of dismissing it and rejecting it, she learned to acknowledge it and actually give herself the attention, acceptance and love she had always wanted and needed.

So many of us find ourselves in a similar situation to Amy's without really understanding why. One thing I've learned, however, is that all human beings long to be free and whole. We're all longing for the same things, whether consciously or subconsciously. But if we search 'out there' for our freedom and wholeness, while rejecting who we actually are, we end up more trapped and incomplete than before.

There's nothing 'out there' that will ever give you a sense of your own worth and wholeness. As an act of unconditional self-love, then, you must shift your gaze from out there to inside, to meet the real longing you hold within you. Through this courageous step you're actively saying to yourself: 'I am ready to meet myself and hear myself and allow myself to receive what I truly long for. I am now ready to allow myself to be fulfilled.' This is not easy, it is not without pain, and it will not give you an instant high of 'feeling better', but it will open up the possibility of experiencing a much deeper fulfilment and wholeness within yourself. A wholeness you can embrace and embody; one that can guide your life choices from that moment on.

We consciously choose to step off the hamster wheel as an act of love, and to honour our true authentic selves.

As Amy surrendered and stopped striving, as she learned to just *be* with her unworthiness, she allowed the possibility of deeper maturation. She began to see that no one was to blame in this scenario. Her father had grown up in a poor family and had few material things as a child; in fact, he often never knew where his next meal would come from. As a result, he grew up with a feeling of lack and survival imprinted within him. He'd worked extremely hard to gain financial security in his twenties and associated having money, material things and abundant food on the table with his own survival. As Amy and I explored her father's story more deeply, his behaviour began to make perfect sense. It had never really been about her, it had nothing to do with her worth or value; he was just doing the best he could with what he had. In fact she realized that, in his own way, he had actually loved her very, very much.

This understanding allowed Amy to find a deeper compassion for herself. She realized that the more accepting and present she is with all of who she is, the more true happiness and fulfilment comes. She now has a much more honourable relationship with herself and her emotional and soul needs, with a commitment to be there unconditionally for herself and with herself. She's learned to create within herself that safe, holding, grounding connection she longed for, which has allowed her true authenticity to begin emerging through. She's now following what her heart truly wants and dreams of by embarking on a new career path.

What Do You Really Want?

Within you is a deep emotional human need and I want to invite the possibility that it is one you may not be aware of or that you don't know how to meet or support. Trying to fix it with anything other than what you *really* want is only going to create more and more suffering for you. So let's shift the gaze from 'out there' and look within you. Let's get to the root of what it is you may actually want and need, and how this may have been dictating so much of the unfolding of your life up till now.

EXERCISE: LOOKING WITHIN

1. Write down a list of all the ways in which you have tried to solve your problems so far. Get super-honest with yourself. For example: *Go to gym to sculpt my body so I can finally feel worthy about myself. Dumped my boyfriend and got a new one to stop feeling lonely. Changed my job to get away from being stressed and panicky only to be stressed and panicky in the new job.* Make the list as exhaustive as you can. We cannot heal what we cannot see, so the more you write down, the more you are seeing – and opening the doorway to change and healing.

2. Looking at this list, ask yourself: has any of it truly worked? Has it really given you what you wanted in a way that lasted?

Write down a few paragraphs describing the pattern that usually occurred. For example: *Felt great at first but then the same old struggle started slipping back in.*

3. Now describe how this may have caused even more problems for you than before.

4. Are you willing to admit now that maybe this way hasn't worked? Can you see that you've been trying to solve problems with the same problem, which has ended up causing problems?

'TUNING IN' MEDITATION

Close your eyes and take three deep breaths in. As you exhale, just release, slowing right down and bringing your awareness inwards.

Choose a recent situation when you were trying to solve a problem with the same problem. Now become really present to yourself and how you felt as you were trying to solve the problem. Breathe deeply and slowly.

Ask yourself this question: what do I really want? What do I really want?

Allow space for the answer to come to you and when it does, really listen. (Remember back to your decision to trust?) The answer may not initially make any sense to you, but think: what have you really wanted?

After some time, and when you feel clear, bring your awareness back to the present and allow your breathing to regulate as you slowly open your eyes.

Write in your journal what came to you. Was it love? Worth? Safety? Security? Belonging? Spend some time describing in your journal what you saw and heard.

If you didn't hear anything, you may need to practise this meditation daily for a few weeks as you awaken your sensitivity to tune in to your deeper needs. This is absolutely fine: remember your commitment to being patient and compassionate with yourself.

Write a few paragraphs journalling about what you truly want and whether the ways in which you've been trying to get it have actually been meeting with any success. Allow yourself to sit with this want within you – without yet knowing how to solve it – first just to allow yourself to see it, honour it, be with it.

This is your core need.

Surrender to Not Knowing

When any of us is given the invitation, 'Do you want to break free of your patterns and live more empowered and free?', every single one of us will immediately say, 'Yes, yes, yes', without ever considering what that really means. This is one of the greatest misconceptions when it comes to transforming who we are being and how we are living.

If I were to ask you, here and now, 'Are you now ready to break free of your patterns and suffering so you can live empowered, joyful and free in your life?', what would your immediate answer be? It's 'yes', right? Without even a moment's thought? Of course that's your answer, because who doesn't want that? Because what sits alongside that answer is often a perception that, once you get to live in freedom, empowered and free, everything will be better. Everything will be good and peaceful and it'll be easy being you. You'll sit alongside God feeling full of euphoria and shining your beautiful light on the world.

Such a pretty, beautiful picture. And one that is not remotely aligned with truth. Sorry. This is the picture that's sold to us as a beautiful marketing 'sell', but it's not the truth.

To break free of our patterns, to embody our most authentic, empowered and free selves, requires us to surrender – surrender everything we think we know about who we are and how we should be living our life. The beliefs, ideas and survival strategies; the behaviours, patterns and programming that have dictated how we have lived our lives up to now. Led by unhealed trauma from our past, fuelled by the stories we have identified with in our minds, but none of which have anything to do with what is real in the here and now – none of which is who we truly are.

This is not an easy ask and it takes remarkable courage of heart – to surrender what we know, even if what we know is causing us pain, even if that suffering at least gives us some sense of control and security. As opposed to diving head first into the complete unknown, consciously leaving behind that false sense of security, in service of what is authentic and true. That requires great bravery.

For now, take a moment to think about what you do 'know' – about who you are; about what you need in order to get what you want; about all of your life, in fact. Where did you learn what you 'know'? Think about it. Everything you think you know about yourself and your life has been inherited from someone or somewhere else. *Everything*.

The ideas and beliefs of who you are as a woman or man. The patterns, the ways of behaving in life, in intimacy. Even the language you speak. All inherited from parents, teachers, friends, society. The ideas of what is the 'right' way and the 'wrong' way for you to live your life. The options you feel you have, and choices you feel you should be making, in order to 'be loved' or 'acceptable'. Every single view you have about who you are – who you are meant to be, how you are meant to live your life, what is required of you in order to be loved or unloved or worthwhile or not – has been given to you by someone else, and was given to them by someone else, and to those before them by someone else. And if every single view is simply programming, but nothing is original or authentic, then what is true and what isn't?

In this moment I'd like to invite you to ask yourself the following question and, as you do so, take a moment to be still and to reflect on what this question offers: what do you actually know *for certain*?

Your maturation and healing are about unlearning what you 'know' – what you've been programmed with that is blocking your ability to see who you are and to see clearly, full stop. Everything you know, everything that's got you to where you are right now, might indeed have served a purpose in many ways. As you're here with me reading this book, however, I'm assuming that such knowledge hasn't given you what you hoped it would give you.

Surrendering to the not-knowing is scary because we latch on to our need to know under the vain illusion that knowing gives us more control. Yet the more we 'know', the less free we are. To consciously choose to go to a place in which we are guaranteed to feel lost and out of control, however, is quite a daunting decision to make. Because it can feel like a death. A death of the identity you thought you had, of who you thought you were.

So why do you think it would be worth making such a choice? Because on the other side of all that you know is the unknown, and all possibility, authenticity and truth exists there. Because living aligned with authenticity and truth opens up a new possibility for your life, with a much deeper sense of connection, purpose, worth and consciousness. And after you've tried this other way for a while – living on the hamster wheel versus living connected, alive and awake – well, there's really no trade-off. Remember: you were born not just to get by, but to live and thrive.

Regardless, however, it's not easy. Not at all. And I feel it is much more valuable for you and me and us to truly own that it is not easy; that if we are to make this choice, we make it in the full awareness of what our choice entails; that we go in with fully open eyes and a full, open heart; that we are consciously choosing our freedom over what is easy and comfortable.

That in itself is immensely empowering and healing.

The Death of the Warrior Woman

When I returned from the jungle, the only truth I knew was that I was no longer willing to continue neglecting and abandoning myself or continue these repeated patterns from my childhood. I knew something had to change, but I had no idea what. I trusted enough that, if I kept staying aligned with my truth, what needed to be done and what needed to happen would be made clear to me.

Your maturation is about unlearning

what is blocking your ability to see

who you truly are. Surrendering

to the 'not-knowing' is your

pathway to becoming free.

~

Within a week of me returning home, the same old fight started to kick off between my husband and me. But this time something remarkable happened that had never happened before. As my husband became triggered and angry, doing what he had always done, instead of reacting as I usually would – fighting back and feeling abandoned – I felt no trigger at all. In fact, I felt so calm and grounded that I simply stayed sitting quietly in my chair and didn't say a word. As I sat there in my stillness, not reacting, all that was left was my husband doing his part of the dance on his own. As I, calm in my chair, witnessed him in his anger, I saw for the first time that his reactions, his behaviour and his anger had nothing at all to do with me (after all, I wasn't doing anything except sitting and breathing). In fact, I saw beyond his behaviour and saw his hurt, his pain and his heart: it was all his and I couldn't fix it.

It was a huge 'aha!' moment.

I realized something in that moment, about all the hopes I'd held on to for fixing our marriage: how if I was just more successful, more beautiful, kinder, more tolerant, more something-other-than-who-I-am, maybe – just maybe – the dynamic between us could resolve itself. But now, for the first time in our nine years together, I was ready to surrender and let go; to let go of trying to get him to see me, hear me, not abandon me. All the same ways I had lived and behaved as a child with my mother. I let go of trying to control where I had no control and I brought the focus solely on to honouring my truth. By the next morning, I knew I was ready to let the struggle come to an end, and with that came the end of our marriage. He moved out a week later.

Consciously choosing to let our marriage die, without having any plan in place for what to do next or where it would lead, was one of the most courageous (and painful) choices I've ever made in my life. But I did it because living aligned with my authenticity and truth meant more to me than holding on to something that was causing so much suffering – even though it offered security and certainty too. Little did I know that making that choice to surrender so deeply to the complete unknown ended up leading me into one of the most transformational periods of my life.

As my marriage died, my understanding of who I'd known myself to be died with it. I'd spent my whole life feeling that I had to be a strong, confident woman; fighting to be seen, fighting to be heard, with a powerful need to prove myself. It was such a painful way to live, because I never felt safe enough to allow myself to rest or let go, to allow myself to just *be*. I'd been trying so hard to survive – survive the trauma of my childhood, survive the addiction, survive, survive, survive – my whole identity had been built on being a survivor. Yet now, for the first time in my entire 40 years, I started to recognize that in all my surviving I had not truly been living.

This way of being had enabled me to get through some incredibly painful experiences in my life, but it had robbed me of so much too. I'd often take on much more than I could handle, becoming completely overwhelmed, drained and ultimately resentful. Always overworking, pushing myself so hard all the time in the hope that I could prove my worth and value. Always supporting others – being strong for people, being there for them – yet often inside feeling so alone and unsupported myself. And feeling that no one would ever be strong or safe enough to actually support me.

I had no idea how much this way of living was draining me until after my husband left when, just as I realized that I was ready to let my marriage die, I recognized too that I was ready to let the warrior woman die. Surrendering all this was a deeply vulnerable, raw and scary process. But my intention to live aligned with truth and authenticity kept calling me through. Answering my calling home to the Nicky that was there – whole, complete and already enough – long before the survival strategy of being the warrior had ever even begun. This meant much more to me than holding on to what I thought I'd known.

What Do You Know for Certain?

Such a powerful question. When you explore it deeply, it has the power to expand you beyond the programming of who you considered yourself to be and what you thought your life was. Everything you think you know about yourself, everything you think you know about the world, is based on assumptions, beliefs and opinions that were taught or told to you as true. Yet until you allow yourself to question what you think you know for sure, and surrender to the unknown, you can never allow yourself to expand into the limitless possibility of who you truly are – which, if you remember, is what you said you actually wanted to do. Remember? 'Are you now ready to break free of your patterns and struggle so you can live empowered, joyful and free in your life?' And you answered, 'Yes!'

As soon as we allow ourselves to ask 'What do I know for certain?', we realize we know absolutely nothing, and I actually mean *know* rather than think. And thus we dive into the wilderness phase: the lostness, the space in between who we once knew ourselves to be and who we have not yet become. The phase when the caterpillar has disappeared into the cocoon but not yet emerged as the butterfly.

And you may say to yourself, 'I don't know who I am', 'I feel so lost', or 'I don't know anything any more' – but if you find yourself saying these words, don't fall into a pit of despair. Instead, celebrate, rejoice and be proud of yourself and your journey. Because you're now on the pathway home to your authenticity and truth, which can only begin from the unknown. You've been courageous enough to surrender and trust even when it's seemed impossible. And that is a remarkably courageous act indeed.

EXERCISE: INQUIRING INTO THE UNKNOWN

1. Focus your attention on the biggest problems and complaints you have already written about in the previous exercises. For each of these problems and complaints, ask yourself the question: 'What do I know for certain?'. Describe in your journal what occurs for you as you apply this question to each issue.

2. After every answer you give, ask the question again: 'Do I *really* know this for certain?' Do you *know* it? Or were you just taught it, shown it, told it?

3. With the intention to allow the question to drop to a deeper place beyond your mind, I invite you to close your eyes and take two deep breaths in, each time exhaling slowly. Then, as you allow your breathing to return to its natural rhythm, ask yourself: 'What do I know for *certain*?' Let the question sit in your space as you continue to breathe slowly and deeply into your body and out. *What do I know for certain?* Allow the question to apply to your entire life and self.

4. Keep asking the question and allow yourself to let the question move through you as you reflect on who you have known yourself to be in the past and how you need to be living your life going forwards.

'LETTING GO' MEDITATION

Close your eyes and take three deep breaths into your being – each time counting slowly to eight as you breathe in and eight as you exhale. As you breathe, allow your body to relax and your attention to be brought to meet yourself in the present moment.

Now return to breathing in a natural rhythm – allow your body to breathe itself. Bring your attention to your life as you live it right now. Focus on the material world you have right now: your house, your clothes, your kitchen – what you have been taught about whether or not you need these things. This has all been taught to you by outside sources. Everything you know about what material things you need and why you need them has been passed on to you by others. And so… let it go.

Bring your attention to your body: your stomach, thighs, arms, cheeks, nails – everything you have been taught about your own body. What is beautiful, not beautiful, acceptable, unacceptable – even what the names of your body parts are – has all been inherited from others, and others before them. Let it all go.

Bring your attention to who you know yourself to be: your job, status, your role as a partner, a mother – whatever 'labels' seem to apply. All these definitions of who you are have been passed on to you by others, and others before them. Let it all go.

Bring your attention to your gender, your skin colour, your nationality: male, female, non-binary, white, black, Asian, British, American. All these labels, names, ideas have been inherited from others, and others before them. Let it all go.

Bring your attention to language, to the words you use. It is inherited from others. Let it go.

Bring your attention to yourself and who you think you are. Let it go. Let it all go.

And now simply breathe into this sense of space. Where are you now? Just sit and breathe and be in this space of stillness, quietness and immense possibility. Imagine living your life from this space. Imagine creating from this space. Sit here and let yourself breathe for a few moments.

When you feel ready, open your eyes.

Describe in your journal your experience of the above meditation and what comes to you while being in this place of spaciousness.

CHAPTER 2

Living Beyond the Story

'We do not see the world as it is, we see it as we are.'

ANAÏS NIN

L et me tell you the story of the frog in the well. There's this frog, and he lives in a well. He has lived his whole life in this well, and all he knows is this well. In fact, this well is his whole world, and he has no perception of the possibility of anything else. Then, one day, he learns to jump, because that is the nature of a frog, and each day he jumps a little higher than before, until one day he jumps so high that his head pops above the top of the well. As his head pops over the top of the well, he catches a glimpse of a huge, vast, enormous world beyond this well – a world he didn't know existed. And it is so huge it takes his little frog breath away.

Then he falls back into the well.

Yet now the world he's known has shifted. Everything has changed, yet nothing is different. But now, he has seen another possibility; a world beyond the walls of this well. For the first time in his life he looks at the walls that surround him – walls that he has only ever seen as 'just his world' – and he begins to see them as walls, and ones within which he is trapped. And all he longs for now is his freedom, even though only a few moments before, he never actually considered himself as not already free. His freedom is to live beyond the walls of this well. His freedom lies not in getting rid of the well, abandoning the well, or even vacating it completely. But to *know* in every part of his froggy being that the well is *not* who he is and it is *not* his world.

You are the frog in the well.

Except the well in which you are currently captive is the narrative of a story with which you have identified and which you are currently calling your life. Your attachment to and identification with this story are the walls that are confining you and your freedom.

The first step towards becoming *free* is to see that you are not in fact free at all. To see clearly that you are in fact the opposite of free; you are trapped. You are in a well. Your life – how you are, all the struggles and problems and suffering you keep finding yourself in – these are not 'just the way it is'. You are *in a story* in which you are the *main character* and that story itself *is the well* that has disguised itself as what you have come to believe is your life.

The beginning of the frog's journey to freedom *only* begins when he catches a glimpse of a new possibility that completely alters his whole perception of his world and who he is in it. Back in the well, his experience of his whole world has changed. Now he can see he is not a frog just living in his world; he is in a well, and the well has walls, and the walls are blocking him from living in the expansiveness he saw beyond. He now can see that he is not free.

I want you to pause for a moment and look at your life. Choose one of the biggest problems or pain points that you are struggling with right now and, just for a moment, really focus on that particular problem.

What are the specific details or feelings or experiences that are causing the pain?

Now review the whole of your life so far and look for all of the other many times you've experienced this same pain or experience before. The external details will be different, but the internal experience will be the same if you are willing and courageous enough to let yourself see it.

You may just see it for little moments before the awareness disappears, or you may see it and then immediately forget what you've seen. That's okay; that's your brain trying to process this shift in perception. Little moments are good enough for now. But in these little moments, as you see the connections, sequences, repetition, I want you to ask yourself:

'Am I in a story? Am I in a well? One that has coloured how I experience my life?'

Take a moment to let that land. Breathe.

Me and My Well

Throughout most of my life, particularly the first half, I've struggled to believe that I was ever worthy of receiving love and nourishment. I identified so much with being bad, unworthy and 'not enough'. This story coloured my entire world, showing up in every area of my life. I had this internal magnet that would either attract people, places and things that would prove to be painful, unloving, and unavailable to me; or it would repel, so if anything wonderful and nourishing did come along, I'd find a way to sabotage it and push it far away. If it didn't 'fit' with the story with which I identified, I would make sure it wouldn't be part of my life.

Of course this was all unconscious. I truly believed that was just the way it was for me; that was 'just the way life is' and that was just who I was in the world. No matter how much I tried to make things 'better' on the outside, I always ended up back in that same painful place of feeling unworthy.

My father had left my mother before I was born, so she was utterly heartbroken by the time I arrived. Imagine being left by the love of your life while nine months pregnant and with a three-year-old boy and a five-year-old girl already (my brother and sister). As a mother myself now, if I let that reality into my heart I can become overcome with empathy for her pain. By the time I was born, then, my mamma was in the depths of her own depression. I remember feeling very alone as a little girl, as though I didn't belong anywhere or to anyone. I could feel my mother's sadness so deeply and was convinced it must have been due to me. If only I could make her happy – be brighter, more lovable, shinier. I'd literally dance around, performing, singing, bouncing around like a beam of light, in my attempts to alleviate her pain. But it never worked.

As I grew up, the dynamic between us became more and more difficult. The combination of her difficulties as a single mother with her own emotional struggles on top of that, and my ever-growing neediness and desperation to fix her, and be loved and validated, meant I'd often bear the brunt of her anger and frustration.

Very quickly I started to believe there must be something very wrong with me. I must be bad inside. I must be wrong. In my mind, I was the reason she kept being angry and therefore I must be a terrible, unlovable person. This was the narrative I told myself and it was the story I utterly believed was the truth. The impact of trauma is not determined solely by what a child actually experiences physically; it is determined by what is happening internally for that child and what the child makes it all mean, about themselves, as those external circumstances occur.

So when my mother would lose her temper, snap, or get frustrated, angry and reactive towards my neediness, internally I'd feel enormous shame, rejection, heartbreak and a deep sense of failure. I'd tell myself it must be because I was bad and unlovable. Thus my story began, with me as a main character who was bad and unlovable and whose mere presence triggered anger in others. My presence caused others pain. I was not someone who was allowed to be loved or receive good things or experience joy. Being me, as myself, was not going to be okay. And so from a very young age I had already begun to seek ways in which I could hide and mask my true self and present a bigger, better, more 'lovable' version of myself.

Thus was my well built. And here's the twist – I was the one who built it. I told myself that story and I made myself the main character. And then I believed it to be the truth and I created the unfolding of my life in a way that matched the story perfectly.

Let me ask you this: was my mother's pain and sadness and anger really about me? Or was she just doing the best she could, being human, muddling on and struggling with her own pain, and it didn't really have anything to do with me? I may have triggered her, but the source of her pain was not about me, it was already there before I came along.

None of it had anything to do with me, but I didn't know that at the time. It took me many decades to finally be able to see and know this – around the same time I became more conscious of the well in which I'd been trapped.

This story I'd told myself had had such a profound impact on me that it had infiltrated every part of the first thirty years of my life. Choosing men that had no ability to offer love or care for me, most of whom had anger issues in some form or other. Hurting my body with bulimia or binge-eating. Chasing oblivion with drugs or alcohol. Sabotaging every dream I ever had.

Only those of us who believe we are worthy of love will allow loving, nurturing relationships in; loving, abundant lives. Only those of us who believe we are unworthy of love will treat ourselves the way I did.

While we're living within the confines of our story and are fully identified with it, however, we simply cannot see these truths. We are blinded. We are blinded by the story itself, knowing only with absolute certainty that it is our reality.

We do not see things as they are. We see things as we are.

Before the frog jumped over the top of the well there was nothing in his perception that knew of a world beyond. And if there is no world beyond the well, then the well in which he lives is just the world. He does not experience it as being captive or not free. He doesn't even call it 'a well'. It is just the reality of his frog life. We do not see things as they are. We see things as we are. And while we remain unaware of the story and identify with it as who we are, we are living our lives blinded without even perceiving that we are blind.

My story was a world in which I was inherently bad inside, which brought out anger in other people and which defined me as unworthy of goodness and love. And my entire life unfolded in perfect support of that story.

Katy's Story

My client Katy was brought up by a violent, alcoholic father. She loved him deeply, but nonetheless he was a violent alcoholic. She'd come into our sessions so frustrated, because she felt that she'd become a magnet for alcoholics in general. In her daily life, she'd often find that they'd sit next to her, or that they seemed to gravitate towards her, which she'd use as evidence to reaffirm that the world was extremely unsafe and that she always had to be on guard. Thus perpetuating the constant state in which she lived as a child.

One day we went for coffee together when a man came to sit at the table next to us and ordered a beer. Within a few minutes, Katy had become very uncomfortable and she turned to me and said, 'There's another one. I should go.' I looked over at the man and all I saw was a nice-looking man in a blue suit with tidy hair having a beer. Katy shared with me that she could smell him the moment he came in, and he smelled just like her father used to smell. And that was it. All she could see was another potentially dangerous, untrustworthy alcoholic.

So it wasn't that she was always attracting alcoholics (although sometimes she did); the story in which she was entrapped was so mechanical that it coloured her world in perfect alignment with it. Katy was still surviving her past. She existed in a story in which she was the victim, always in danger, and that was the reality she experienced every single day. We do not see things as they are. We see things as we are.

One last story. Ten years ago I was a participant in a transformational programme. Sitting in a session, one participant stood up to share how much she couldn't stand me; how enraged and unsafe she felt having me there. She demanded that we were never to work together throughout the programme. I remember that she was physically shaking at the time.

This was an excruciatingly painful experience for me. I'd only met this girl for the first time a few days beforehand, and here I was once again, on the receiving end of a raging woman having a strong reaction to my presence and me not having any idea why or how. This experience was an exact re-enactment of my childhood. My desire to bolt was so intense that my legs were tapping back and forth on the ground. The facilitators of the programme invited me to entertain the possibility that this was happening for a reason; that the pain point occurring for me was the entry point to my deepest healing. I made the commitment to stay. In the next day's group session, I found myself partnered with this girl in a paired exercise. As I sat opposite her, she began literally writhing in anger. And I simply sat there, doing nothing but being with her and breathing. She was having a visceral reaction to me, even though she didn't know me and I was doing nothing but sit there. It was crystal clear that her rage had nothing to do with me. It couldn't have; I was doing nothing, just sitting there while she was having a full-on emotional reaction. She wasn't actually seeing me; she was seeing another version of her own mother. She was seeing me through the lens of her story.

That was the moment in which my head, like the frog's, popped over the top of my own metaphorical well. For the first time in my life, I could see that my mother's rage had nothing to do with me. It was all hers. In that moment my whole world shifted. I am not bad; I am not unworthy. My body began to tingle, I felt a rush of energy move through me, and I experienced a moment of deep peace, freedom and connection: the attachment to my story was dissolving and beginning to release. You see, the world you are living in is not happening to you. It is happening through and from you. We do not see things as they are. We see things as we are. And so the story you have been identifying with is always colouring how you know yourself and how you experience life. But it is a story. One that you wrote, in which you are the main character. But it is not who you are.

Exercise: Looking for Themes

1. Scan back through your life and look at the recurring themes. In your journal, describe in detail the elements that keep repeating themselves over and over again. Those 'details' may be different on the outside, but somehow the way you're experiencing them internally will be the same, no matter how you've tried to change things on the outside.

2. Write a list of all those recurring moments. Ask yourself: at the heart of each moment, what experience was moving through you? What's the recurring belief or story that is showing up in all these moments? For example: *I am the one that's not*

chosen, I am rejected. And the story is that I am unworthy and unlovable; or I am the one who is strong, dominant, in control, running the show, but I am alone and then I am burnt out. And the story is that it is not safe for me to receive. It is not safe for me to trust.

3. If you're struggling to find the common thread, go back through all the recurring problems or issues in your life and for each one write down the story, experiences and beliefs that were coming up. At the end of the exercise, look through them all and go deeper to see what the underlying story is.

'REGRESSION' MEDITATION

Close your eyes and take three deep breaths, simply allowing your body to let go as you exhale. Slow, spacious, conscious breaths.

Bring your awareness inwards and meet yourself.

Become present with a time recently in your life in which you were strongly experiencing a heightened trigger or felt as though you were having a big breakdown. Maybe you were in the middle of a fight with your partner, or triggered by your boss, or even triggered by yourself? I want you to go to that moment and *really* feel it once again.

I invite you to really feel it as though you are there right now.

Then ask yourself these questions:

~ Where is it in my body?

   Is it in your heart, your chest, your stomach?

~ What does this experience feel like?

> *Does it feel like being rejected, unable to trust, or unsafe, or like you're about to be abandoned or attacked?*

~ What does the experience of it in my body feel like?

> *Is it hot, is it cold, is it tight, is it contracting?*

~ Does it have a shape?

~ Does it have a colour?

~ What feelings are attached to it?

> *Are you, for example, feeling anger, sadness, fear, shame, terror, rage, guilt, confusion, numbness, grief?*

~ Do I have a childhood memory of experiencing the exact same thing?

> *What's the first thing that comes to mind?*

~ In this memory, where exactly am I?

~ How old am I?

~ Is it morning, afternoon or evening?

~ What's happening?

Within the moment of that memory, feeling what you are feeling, ask yourself: what decision did I make about myself or about life in this memory?

Go with the first thing that comes to mind.

It's normally something that you are not: *I'm not good enough, I'm not lovable, I'm not worthy, I'm not safe, I'm not able to share myself, I'm not wanted.*

What decision did you make in that moment about yourself or about life?

And as you see that decision, can you see how often it shows up again in your life?

Can you see how that decision colours your world today? Allow yourself to scan through your life and to achieve that awareness.

When you're ready, bring your breathing back to a normal rhythm.

Bring your awareness back to the moment.

And when you're ready, open your eyes.

EXERCISE: BE THE FROG

After doing the meditation above, use your journal to capture whatever you need to from the experience. Then use those notes about your story, your memory, as the starting point for this exercise.

1. Write down 4–5 examples of how this story has influenced things in your life, affected decisions you've made, or determined your behaviour. Allow yourself to really see clearly how the story shows up throughout your whole life, as if you are wearing 'story-coloured glasses'.

2. Continue writing down other incidents and experiences in your life in which this story has coloured how you saw things and how you knew yourself.

3. Is it now super-clear? This story is the well you have been in. You are the frog. The well is not the whole world you thought it was. There is a possibility to live beyond the well. The story doesn't have to define how you live your life.

Surviving Versus Living (or Alive-ing)

My client Tracy lived in a continuous state of stress and panic. Every time she tried to do anything good or nourishing for herself, she was consumed by guilt and shame. Hyper-vigilant in work and life, acutely aware at all times, she truly believed the stress was caused by the years she'd spent working in publishing. She quit her job to work in the world of wellness, but that didn't take the stress away. So she started following a really strict health regime, but that didn't take away the stress either.

No matter what she tried, the stress followed her everywhere. As a result of our sessions, she was able to recognize that she lived in a world in which she expected things to fall apart at any moment. Tracy believed that her stress was caused by the circumstances of her life – the external factors. In fact, however, the experience of stress and chaos were trapped within her.

When Tracy was a little girl, her parents had divorced. She'd felt trapped in the middle, thinking she had to choose who to love more. Internally she would panic at the thought of getting it wrong and causing pain to either parent. Deep at the root of it all, too, she was terrified that if she got it wrong she'd have no one and her whole world would crumble. She was stuck in a story from her past that was keeping her in a loop of survival. But survival has nothing to do with living. Survival is only about 'not dying'.

Tracy was not in her life. She was in her past.

This is the first thing I want you to see. What may be at the core of the patterns that are causing you the greatest suffering is not happening 'out there'; it is happening 'inside you', colouring how you experience 'out there'. And the part that is looping on repeat is not of the present; it is led by the past.

So now I have another question for you: is it life that keeps bringing you situations that coincidentally bring up the same repeated pain points? Or are you bringing those repeated pain points to your life? Tracy was the only consistent factor across all the life experiences that 'made her' stressed. Life wasn't making her stressed: she was bringing the stress inside her (from the past) to her present life. When we are stuck in the past, we are not present in the now. And the now is the only moment that exists – the only moment when authentic life flows.

Surviving is simply getting through, coping, 'not dying'. But living is being free.

We can only live if we are present in the moment. So living is just not available to us if we remain stuck in the story.

My mentor David used to lead maturation programmes in high-security prisons in the USA. On one occasion, as he was being led through the main cell block to the workshop space – walls of small barred cells all around him, covering two whole floors – he noticed one particular cell. In that cell, the inmate had pasted every single wall with wallpaper images of a beautiful green forest. The entire cell was covered by

You don't need to be trapped

in survival any more.

Your freedom is calling you.

You are and always have been

the one with the power.

~

wall-to-wall green forest imagery. It was beautiful to see. The guards explained that that particular inmate was going to be in prison for the rest of his life: a 'lifer' with no parole. As David prepared to begin the workshop, he realized something: that inmate was doing the best he could to make his life better, to make it more comfortable, more endurable, nicer. He was doing the best he could to make the most of it.

But no matter how much 'better' he made it, he wasn't free.

This is survival.

And if we're doing this with our lives, we aren't really living, we're just surviving – which is a way of being that is distinct from living. We hope that if we keep pasting up different wallpaper to make it look and feel better, we'll get by, we'll cope, we'll get through. But we are not free. Living free is to be in the presence of your experience of life. Surviving is to be in the story about your experience of life, thus removing you from the living of it.

To truly live, therefore, we need to be here now, in the present, with ourselves as we are, with life and all that arises. We cannot survive and live at the same time. So I have good news for you, and I have not-so-good news for you, and of course I'm going to tell you both.

The good news is: you don't need to be trapped in survival mode any more. Your freedom is calling you. It is possible for you to dissolve your attachment to the story, thus breaking free from that cycle of surviving and starting to truly live. Even here in this moment, as you read this and see it for what it is, you're already opening the gateway to your freedom and peace.

The not-so-good news is this: I cannot be the one to dissolve your attachment to your story and therefore I cannot get you 'out of the well'. Not just because, if I did, it would rob you of realizing so much of your own power. But also because I actually can't. You are the one – the *only* one – who can get yourself out of the well. You can learn from teachers, be guided, gain insight, have powerful epiphanies, even have huge experiences of peace and freedom and 'feeling better'. When it comes down to it, however, it is *you* who must go into your own life and integrate what you learn and see and gain, and through your own growing awareness, *you* will be the one who begins dissolving the walls of your own well and shifting the reality in which you know yourself and in which you stand.

This is going to have to come from you. You are and always have been the one with the power.

I'm going to teach you how to see your story and how to understand that you are the author of the story and how to recognize when you are in the story. I'll show you how to see that you are not your story, and how to be so loving and compassionate with yourself in it that you no longer need the story. But at the end of the day, my love, you must go do it and live it yourself, in order for you to truly discover your own power, your own truth and your own freedom.

Dissolving Attachment

The well is not the problem. The story is not the problem. Your attachment to the story is the problem.

Tracy didn't see her stress as an experience that she carried within her, attached to a moment in time from her past. If she did, she'd have been able to recognize that, each time it arose within her, it had nothing to do with her present moment and no connection to her reality.

If she did, then it would have no power over her whatsoever. She would still be free.

Instead, Tracy only knew that stress as who she was. She knew it as her life. In fact, she was so identified with it that when it wasn't there she felt uneasy and lost. No matter how much she claimed she wanted to get rid of this pattern, it was all she'd ever known. Tracy was so attached to this pattern that even when she tried to change things, she always set it up so that she'd find herself back at what she already knew: stress. To step out of survival and allow herself to live – to become peaceful, joyful, rested and free – she would have to own her attachment to the story and to survival, and be willing to let it go. Surrender.

The moment at which we distinguish the story as a story and the survival as a reaction to the story, and how attached we are to the surviving, is the moment we loosen the grip of our attachment to the story itself. Creating enough space between our awareness and the story to open the possibility of living differently.

EXERCISE: WHAT'S YOUR STORY?

1. In your journal, write down an exhaustive list of all the ways you've been trying to run away or resist the story that's been defining your life. In what ways have you been putting up wallpaper and convincing yourself it's enough? For example, my story is: *I'm not worthy as I am. I've spent my life trying to be better than everyone else, to be a complete overachiever. I had*

to be the star of the show; I had to be the loudest, the prettiest, the skinniest. To prove to the world I was worthy, because deep down I believed I wasn't. But whenever anything good came into my life – a good man, a happy friendship, money in my bank account – or whenever I got close to realizing a dream, I'd sabotage it all. As then I'd have the evidence that I'm right, I am indeed not worthy. Even if it's not completely obvious to you, keep writing and exploring, hold the question and the inquiry with you as the insight slowly comes to you more and more. Then write what you see in your journal to capture it.

2. What is your greatest fear? What strategies have you adopted to avoid ever experiencing that fear? Dig as deep as you can go here. What's the big boogieman fear that lives at the heart of everything you do in your life? Bring it out of the shadows and into the light. For me it's the fear of being completely unloved and rejected and abandoned, with this story at the heart: *I am unworthy.* I created a whole persona to make sure I was liked, loved, and in control: the warrior woman. It was a survival strategy and did not work.

3. Describe what your survival strategy has given you and what it continues to give you. For example: *It allows me to stay a victim so others will take care of me. It allows me to feel in control.*

4. Now write a list of what holding on to survival will *rob* from your life going forwards. Please be courageous here. Remember, you are the only one who can get yourself out of this.

5. Lastly, now that you have written these lists… are you ready to consider surrendering these survival strategies?

Reaction Versus Response

As you sit with the question of surrendering your survival, let's take this another step further. Let me ask you: what's the difference between a reaction and a response? Take time to reflect on a recent moment in your life when you were obviously 'reacting' to something rather than responding. Then reflect on a moment in your life when you were clearly responding rather than reacting.

It would be perfectly normal for there to be no example of responding yet; maybe you can't even tell the difference. That's absolutely okay, because that's why you're here: to start seeing things you couldn't see before. We think we're just 'living our life', but while we are in the story we are not living; our story is living us, and we are blind to it – we have story-coloured blinkers on our eyes.

And that is the difference between reaction and response.

When we live in reaction, we're taking actions without being able to 'see' clearly. We're acting blindly, subconsciously, on default, without any deliberate choice. A reaction is what it says on the tin: a re-action; an action repeated automatically over and over again. It is mechanical and it happens as it always happens, without conscious choice involved. It has a certain quality about it that is overpowering and it compels us. When we are in reaction, we are hijacked by our past and mostly without knowing it. When we're stuck in the story, we're stuck in the past, and actions led by the past are automatically going to repeat the past. In order to have active choice, we need to be present and conscious in the moment. Consciousness is to be awake and present in the moment – something that is not possible when our past is contaminating our present. When reactions occur that are led by survival – led by the past – the only result that can unfold is a repeat of our past. We are stuck in survival led by our past; our reactions are dictated by this survival strategy (even as we are think we are living), which creates more results aligned with the story of the past, reinforcing it and keeping us trapped in survival. We just go round and round on the hamster wheel, hoping that one day things will change. We're no different to the frog, moving to different parts of the well over and over again in an attempt to create a new life, but all the time remaining stuck in the well. *Re*-actions will never create a new possibility for your life. Re-actions can only re-enact what occurred in your past. Re-actions will never allow you off the hamster wheel.

So what is response? Response is what becomes possible when we pop our head over the top of the well; when the blinkers come off, even for a millisecond. Response is action following conscious choice. And to be able to choose from a conscious place, we need to be able to stand beyond the story. We need to be awake and present in the moment and to the story itself. Response is action that creates the possibility not just of getting off the hamster wheel, but of creating a whole life beyond the hamster wheel. Life beyond the story. Only when we are responding to life rather than reacting to it can we create the unfolding of a life beyond the story of the past, because it is not what we do that determines the impact or power of our actions, it is where we are coming from. When we respond rather than react, we are coming from a place that is consciously rooted in the present; aware of the story, and that we have been in a story, but that we are not the story. So let me ask you this: where do actions come from? What is it that leads actions?

Please sit with this question without grasping for an answer while I tell you a story.

Returning from Peru

When I returned from Peru I was able to see more clearly what was occurring in my marriage. That fight we had, when his behaviour followed the usual pattern but I didn't react, was a pivotal moment for me in the marriage. In that moment of not reacting I found myself gaining some of my power back. What seemed like a simple moment of not reacting, while being aware of what was occurring in the present, opened up the unfolding of many new possibilities ahead. Possibilities for conscious responses.

When I asked him to move out, it was painful, it was scary, it broke my heart into a million pieces, but I was conscious when I did it. It was not a reaction; it was a response. I was choosing to participate no longer in that reactive spiral he and I had found ourselves in over and over again. I was consciously choosing to honour and care for my heart, my truth, and my needs. I was consciously choosing to surrender my longing to change him and to focus on what I needed to change in myself. I was consciously choosing to surrender surviving, willing to leap into the unknown in order to discover a new way to live and be. It was the beginning of me showing up for myself, for my life and in my life very differently; coming from a place where I no longer needed to be the warrior woman, pushing and forcing and controlling everything in order to survive and keep myself safe.

After making that choice of asking my husband to leave, I continued to make more conscious choices. I consciously chose to commit to meeting him for therapy every week without knowing what that would mean or where that would take us. I chose to show up even when every part of my body and mind told me to shut down and run away. I chose to allow myself to stop being strong all the time and to be vulnerable, to ask for help from friends, to let myself be supported. I chose to stop participating in the story and to let myself be loved and to let myself not have any answers. I chose to respond even when I didn't know how to do it. And it was painful. I cried and cried a lot. There were nights when I was up alone with the baby and I'd never felt so lonely.

During that time, I felt everything: loneliness, pain, fear, anger, grief, sadness, doubt. But I felt them and they didn't kill me. In fact, I started to see how much of my survival loop and past reactions had been about trying to avoid feeling any of those emotions at all. I was in full surrender. Not surrender of my power, not surrender of my will, but surrender of the fight, surrender of the control, surrender of the walls I had built around myself for far too long, and surrender of my attachment to the story and to the survival. I chose surrendering it all in order to discover how to live more authentically, more aligned and more consciously.

The pain of my husband moving out reactivated the pain of my father leaving when I was a baby. The pain of being a single mother with two very young children, both of whom needed so much attention and energy, brought up the pain of feeling unsupported by my mother. And through *all* this pain I saw more clearly. I saw that, when my husband moved out, my son was exactly the same age I'd been when my father left for good. And that my daughter was exactly the same age as I'd been when my father remarried. I mean: what are the chances of that? The timing was unbelievable, and I knew it wasn't a coincidence. All my years of surviving and reacting had been strategies to avoid feeling and being with all the pain that was now arising. I could see clearly that this was an opportunity to finally change the story and heal.

One gift I took from my conscious choices was to finally learn to be with all I'd been running from my whole life. I couldn't see where it was taking me, but I trusted that this was part of me coming back to life and to myself – my authentic self that had been buried under a lifetime of story. I trusted that, as long as I continued doing my best to *respond* to life rather than *react*, and to consciously make choices aligned with what my truth was, everything would unfold in the way it needed to in order for a new possibility to emerge.

None of it is about getting it right all the time. It's simply about doing our best to just take the next best step, consciously, awake, with sight. Responding. And sometimes we'll realize it didn't feel quite right, or the choice didn't quite give us what we needed, but instead of reacting, we get to respond again. And sometimes the response is to say 'I don't know how to do this', or 'I can't see clearly in this moment so I won't take action', or 'I only know how to react right now so I surrender taking action right now'.

These are all powerful, conscious responses too.

The first step towards being able to respond is to recognize those situations in which we feel unable to respond and find ourselves just reacting. Witnessing the grip or the hold of the story while it is actually gripping. Because if we are able to witness it in the midst of the grip we are not fully overpowered by it. We have some consciousness, and that is the starting point for dissolving its power, and the first step towards being able to respond consciously.

That space between the subconscious reaction and the point at which we are able to at least witness the reaction is where we are first gifted with enough space to begin consciously responding. And the more we can witness, the greater the consciousness, and the more space we have to choose differently.

Responding to life rather than reacting to life is consciously to create our life. A life beyond the story of the past. One where we get to choose who we wish to *be* in our lives. This is the point at which we can live with much more power, much more alignment and much more truth.

EXERCISE: RECOGNIZING REACTION

1. In your journal, list five examples of occasions when you were triggered and had no control over how you were feeling or behaving, or what was coming out of your mouth. Expand on the details: what was happening in your body; what were you feeling; what were you thinking, saying, doing? How did you feel afterwards? What was the impact it had on your life afterwards? And was there a familiar pattern to all these experiences?

2. Having explored more deeply the story that has been living you (the well in which you are the frog), ask yourself whether this story was at the root of some, if not all, of these reactive experiences? Write down how and why.

3. Having recognized these reactive moments in time, can you see how they may be coming up in multiple areas and times in your life – both in the past and today?

4. What part of your past is this reaction replaying?

5. When you're in the reaction, how old are you? What are you convinced you're seeing compared to what is actually there? Are you open to the possibility that you are being blinded by

the past? For each of the five examples you've listed in Step 1, write down one alternative perception – a different interpretation of events that could have been happening instead of what your reaction was telling you.

'Being With' Meditation 1

There'll be times when the emotional memory of the past is triggered within you and instantly puts you into a reactive state. This is the time to strengthen your ability to *be with* the experience that is moving through your body, to *hold* it within you before acting – each time allowing a greater and greater pause before behaviour. This is what transforms a reaction into a conscious response. And this is what starts creating a new possibility.

Sit in a comfortable position and take three big, deep breaths in, allowing the exhale to be a simple release, slowing right down.

Bringing your awareness into the present. Here and now.

Now think of the biggest, most recent of the five reactive experiences you listed in the above exercise. Bring to the fore the feelings and experience that came up at the heart of the trigger. Amplify them to the max.

Observe where the trigger sits in your body and make a mental note of that. Notice how its energy feels. Is it heavy? Tight? Contracting? Fluttery? Notice whether it has a colour or a shape. Notice what feelings are attached to it. Notice how old you are in the experience. Is there a memory attached to this? Allow in the first answer that comes to mind.

And, as you see the answers come... simply *be with it. Be wholly with it.* No escaping, no running away, no distraction. *Be with it fully.* If emotions come, let them come and let them go. Simply sit and *be with it*, without trying to fix it, change it, or make it go away.

Try to sit and be with it for as long as you can: 10 minutes; 20 minutes. Notice if it starts to move, or even to dissolve.

When you are done, bring your awareness back to the moment and open your eyes. Describe in your journal any insights or 'aha!' moments that came to you. Practise this meditation daily to gain more power over the past.

BODYWORK: PHYSICALLY BEING

Another extremely powerful form of practice can help you *be* more with the emotional memory that moves through you. This is to create a pause before reaction, using bodywork, or body movement. Not the same as doing movement *to* your body, this is moving *with* your body – with awareness, consciousness, presence, connection and engagement.

For the next 7–10 days, commit to practising some form of bodywork every day for a minimum of 30 minutes. Be sure to choose a form of bodywork that will invite you to engage more with your body rather than to vacate it: suitable options include, for example, yoga, walking, breathing, dancing, running, shaking, self-massage.

Seeing with New Eyes

When we speak of 'seeing' things, we commonly think of what we see right in front of us, but do we ever really question where it is that we are 'seeing' from? I mean: we can't get behind our eyes and see what is projecting what we see, can we? While we are stuck in the story of survival we are only able to see from the place of the story. The frog at first could only see the reality in which he existed: he didn't see walls, he saw his whole world; he didn't see a well, he saw what for him was life.

When we begin to penetrate the veil that is created by the survival story and stop viewing life through our story-coloured glasses, we begin to see the story, we begin to see the veil, we begin to see the survival. But then we can go even deeper than this. We can begin to see where we have been seeing *from*. To access the power, consciousness and awareness required to dissolve your attachment to the story and walk yourself free, you'll need to learn to see with new eyes – to see differently. Not just looking at what is in front of you, but seeing where you are looking from, seeing while questioning what it is that is being seen, and who is seeing. As I say to my clients: 'Most human beings look only with their eyes, but what I'm inviting you to do is to see with your whole being – your body, your heart, your intuition – with awareness and consciousness and inquiry'.

Becoming 'the Watcher'

Many spiritual teachings describe this process as a fundamental part of living from a more empowered, conscious place as a human being. I use the word 'empowered' not because this process will make you

To create a new path we
cannot rely on memory, as
memory is only the past.

We must begin to see
beyond what we know.

We must see with new eyes.

~

stronger in the conventional sense, but because when you act only from a subconscious, reactive place you lose so much power. With every moment of blindness to who you are being, how you are living and who you truly are beyond your story, you're losing power. And with every moment of seeing through new eyes, becoming conscious of what you could not see before, you reclaim a little more of your authentic power.

Your next step is to deepen that ability to see more clearly. Seeing with new eyes, deepening your awareness. Watching. Observing what's occurring for you, who you've been being, how you've been seeing things previously, and where you've been seeing from. Without judgement, without trying to fix it, change it, escape it, resist it. Simply to *see* the story. Once you see the story, and who you are in the story, and your attachment to the story, the story no longer has all the power. You cannot watch the story and be consumed in the story in the same moment.

By committing to this practice of self-inquiry, of *being the watcher*, you're choosing to allow the way in which you've always seen things and known things to become an inquiry rather than just a fixed reality. It's the moment when the frog can sit in the well, look at the walls and recognize where he is: 'I'm in a well. Look, here are the walls that are surrounding me. I couldn't really see the walls before, but here they are.' We must learn to see more clearly in order to gain more awareness, which will allow us to make conscious choices and act from a different place – a place beyond our story.

Becoming the watcher will not directly change what is happening 'out there', but it will shift the space in which you're standing, allowing you to begin standing in a space beyond the story.

This is the part that no one else can do for you, the part where you have to take responsibility and commit to learning how to get yourself out of the well. This is the part where you reclaim power. And once you *see* more clearly, you cannot unsee.

We Cannot Heal What We Cannot See

When I came into recovery for my addictions, I said to everyone around me, 'I don't need to be here. I don't have a problem. All my friends drink and take drugs and live like me. I'm just normal.' I couldn't see beyond the well I was in. I fully believed that my life reflected normality and reality. As the months went by, however, I began seeing myself differently and my perspective started to shift. I started to recognize that it wasn't normal to get so drunk that I'd try to jump out of windows naked. I started to *see* that it wasn't normal to be purging with my head down a toilet 12–15 times a day. I started to *see* how much destruction and drama seemed to happen for me wherever I went. With every single moment of conscious seeing, my world shifted on its axis a little bit more. The day I *saw* with wide-open eyes that I was in addiction, I felt as though the scales had fallen from my eyes. The veil had lifted. In that moment, my life changed forever. Every moment from that point onwards, every point of change, began with me first seeing things more clearly.

We cannot heal what we cannot see.

When we're consciously engaging in being the watcher, we're looking at our patterns, behaviours, and reactions with open, inquiring eyes. To do this is to acknowledge – even a little bit – that what we're seeing is not who we are; it's what we've been doing and how we've been

~ 73 ~

being. It's dissolving our identification with the story and the character we had formerly believed represented who we were.

It's transforming the space in which you stand and marks the beginning of your path to freeing yourself from the well.

For now, then, the invitation is simply to commit to a daily (lifetime) practice of becoming the watcher; to watching who you are being and how you are living.

EXERCISE: BECOMING THE WATCHER

1. For the next seven days, adopt a practice of self-inquiry into everything about how you're being, how you're feeling and how you're seeing life. It's particularly helpful to notice times of trigger, or heightened emotion or experience – times when you may feel charged or perhaps the opposite: withdrawn. Bring a compassionate, non-judgemental inquiry into your way of being: *What am I feeling, what is rising within me? What am I seeing and how am I experiencing what I'm seeing? Is what I see really there, or does it have a familiar pattern to it from my story?*

2. When and if you have moments of *seeing clearly* – moments of insight, 'aha!' moments – describe them in your journal so you deepen your awareness around this clarity.

3. Then scan back through your life: are there further tangents when you were having the same or similar seeing and experience?

4. I invite you, if you wish, to continue this exercise beyond the seven days and to dedicate a longer fixed period to it.

BODYWORK: BODY-SCANNING

Every morning, when you first wake up into consciousness, before you get up or pick up your phone or talk to anyone, I invite you to spend 3–5 minutes scanning your body and being with awareness.

The moment you open your eyes and come out of the sleep state, lie flat on your back and scan your awareness over and through you, as follows:

1. Observe: how is your physical body? Scan your whole physical body;

2. Observe: how are you feeling emotionally? Scan your whole emotional being;

3. Observe: how are your thoughts, how is your mind? Scan your being;

4. Observe: any thoughts, any feelings, any ideas, any insights. When you can, jot down in your journal what you notice and see.

CHAPTER 3

Overcoming Stuck-ness

'Sometimes letting things go is an act of far greater power than defending or hanging on.'

ECKHART TOLLE

I have a memory that has stayed with me forever. In my first year of recovery from addiction, I began working with a therapist on the relationship I had with my parents, and in particular on this memory, involving an incident with my father. When I was growing up, my father was my hero. I adored and worshipped him in every way. Even though I saw him only one night a week, he'd show up smiling, full of brightness and love. My father has this ability to make anyone he is with feel like the most important person in his world, and that's how I felt when I was with him.

I realize now that creating the story of him as an idealized hero in my world was the perfect way to protect myself. He'd left us when I was so very young – and I know he had his reasons and I have forgiven him completely – but during this period in my life there was a deep sadness buried within me that I'd still not faced, and this story was my safety buffer against it. I was just at the beginning of my journey through processing the pain I'd felt from this abandonment.

Of course, this was the moment my dad came in to town and wanted to take me out for dinner. Life has this incredible ability to orchestrate such things in order to create opportunities for healing. I hadn't seen him in six months and I was extremely nervous to see him. But I went anyway. And it was very painful. I found myself smiling so hard through the whole dinner, desperate to hide what I was really feeling inside, both from him and from myself. And at the end of dinner he gave me a big hug and whispered in my ear, 'I'm sorry. I've always loved you.'

As I walked away, I had no idea how to process what had just happened. It was like a pressure cooker building up inside me. As I sat on the train home I became hot and fidgety, and when I looked down at my thighs, they seemed to be expanding right before my eyes. I blinked, thinking I was imagining it, but as I looked again there they were, doubling in size. Before I knew it I was obsessing about my weight and my looks, about how much I'd eaten at dinner, berating myself for having eaten a dessert, frantically spiralling into a pit of panic, shame and fear at how devastatingly horrific I was. I was on that train for 40 minutes but I didn't notice: I was lost in a world of obsession and I didn't once think of my dad. I also could not feel even a trace of the pain inside me in relation to him or his abandonment of me. My mind was protecting me from feeling the pain; flooding me with noise, as it had done since I was a little girl, to help me survive such very painful times. I identified with it so deeply that it caused me to see my thighs grow before my eyes. Pulling me deeper and deeper into my own well – my well of not being 'enough' and of being worthless. It took me straight out of the moment: lost in the past and future; hijacked by a deep pull to survive.

The mind is so powerful. But the mind is not actually the problem. It is our identification with it and our attachment to the narrative within it that's the problem. Either we can let the mind have power over us, or we can have power over the mind. So what's the difference?

What Is the Mind?

The mind is the home of records, memory, experiences, thoughts – of what's happened internally as well as externally. Every single piece of information stored in the mind is learned, inherited and programmed from somewhere else, and it is all based on the past. An extremely efficient and powerful machine, the mind has the ability to absorb and retain a lifetime – everything we may have been around, lived and experienced in our environment since the day we were born. Nobody really knows where the mind is actually located. It is not in the brain, yet we can't distinguish the mind from the brain, just as we can't separate the front of our hand from the back of our hand. But we do know that each one of us is a someone who has a mind. So what is its actual function?

In my learnings, the design function of the mind is to survive. And if its design function is to survive, what specific memories or experiences do you think the mind will focus on as particularly significant or important? The memories that relate to some form of threat: the difficult ones, the painful ones from our childhood, or anything that is recorded as a threat to our survival. Essentially: trauma. Gathering as much information as possible about our experiences of pain and trauma from the past is the best way possible to ensure we survive and never go through that again. If we were still living in the days of cave-dwellers, and while out hunting we heard a specific noise rustling in the bushes, the memory stored within our mind that recognized the sound as that of a sabre-toothed tiger nearby would immediately alert us, and we would respond and run without a moment's thought. In essence, then, the mind is incredibly useful. But the first problem is that we are all walking around in our lives recognizing any rustle in the bushes as danger, and we react accordingly to survive.

The problem is not the mind or the fact that we have one. The problem is that we believe we are the mind. We walk around our lives hearing the endless noise of records and warnings from the past – information and programming absorbed by the mind – and we identify with it so much we believe that it's the truth of who we are. We believe that it's our life.

In the memory I shared above, I didn't sit on the train hearing the narrative in my mind as simply a narrative in my mind that was trying to help me survive the pain rising in my body. I believed entirely that it was the truth – the reality in that moment. So it's not the mind that is the problem, but our relationship to it.

The very thing that may determine whether we have a 'good' day or a 'bad' day is entirely dependent on whether we are or are not free of our mind that day. Because the mind is informed by absorbed information that can only be based on the past. When we are stuck in the mind or identified with the mind, we are stuck in the past, which means we are not available to the here and now. And that is the most powerful distraction from being present to life.

You Are Not Your Mind

The first thing you need to do is to come out of blindness and start seeing more clearly. You have been becoming the watcher, bringing 'seeing' to who you have been being, and to where you have been seeing from. And this is an essential part of the process; there is simply no possibility of you becoming free of the well without first seeing. But it is not enough on its own. Next, you need to start actually walking. So the next step to seeing is to understand that you are not your mind, and this is something you need to grasp not just on a conceptual level, but on an experiential level.

So, let's try to do that by playing a little game. If you've believed that you are your mind, can you tell me where you are in there?

Seriously, think of your mind right now. Which part of it is you? Where are you in there? Is there a miniature 'you' somewhere in your brain? Let's peel back your hair and skin (I know it's gross but play along with me anyway). Now, open your brain and have a good root around in there.

Are 'you' in there somewhere? Where is this you that you think of so often? If you are not in there, then where are you? And also, where is the mind? Let's play a little more, because this is fun. Who is it that is playing this game with me? Who is searching for you in the mind? These are invaluable questions: not questions that you need to find the answer to, but questions for you to ask and then inquire into. You and your mind coexist. You cannot watch the mind without a 'you', and you as a human being cannot exist without a mind. We coexist but we are not one. We cannot extract our mind from wherever it is in order for us to have more peace or freedom. We must learn to live alongside it; not as enemies, not entangled, but in a healthy, balanced, mutually respectful relationship.

My Mind and Me

A while ago, I went to a festival with a friend. It was the first time since my marriage break-up that I felt like a single woman again and it felt like I was coming back to life. I danced, basked in the sun, attended workshops, even flirted with a guy.

On the evening of the second day, I had a healing session with a Toltec Elder (as you do) called Tai. I don't know what drew me to work with him, but it was like a moth to a flame. In the session, I had a vision of a golden eagle sitting right on my belly. Then I had a vision that I was the eagle, with enormous powerful wings flying through the sky. Tai whispered in my ear, 'Now is your time to fly. Be free.' I burst into tears. All those years of being trapped on the hamster wheel. All those years of getting stuck in the same fight, the same problems, the same pain. I finally felt free.

As I came out of the session, I felt so affirmed that I'd made the right decision by ending my marriage. And that feeling lasted for a good few hours, until my mind got really noisy. The more I tried to hold on to the 'good' feeling, the louder my mind got: repeating the exact same narrative that had played out in my memory of being on the train all those years before. The next morning, I was devastated.

When I saw Tai and told him what was happening, his words were: 'Your mind is not your enemy. It has been trying to protect you for so long. And it is scared for you to become powerful, because it cannot survive without your past story. Instead of rejecting it, say thank you to it for all the years of protecting. But you don't need that any more.'

I went away and I did what he said. The very moment I said it, my mind went silent – completely still – and stayed like that for quite a while. I'd surrendered the battle with my mind and the gift was silence.

The lesson here isn't to go find yourself a shaman. (I mean, you can – but it won't fix you, I'm afraid.) Even after such a euphoric experience of freedom, your mind will return and it will try to get you back in the well. Because it's purpose is to survive. No matter how evolved you become, the mind will continue doing what the mind does.

So your task is not to find your shaman, to keep seeking the next big experience that will 'save' you. Nor is it to extract the mind, or to have no mind. Your lesson is to learn to be with the mind, without identification, with non-attachment. This is the difference between pasting new wallpaper up or walking free. This is how you can begin reclaiming your power in your life.

You are not your mind and your mind is not your enemy. And you have all the power, if you choose to live it. The noise will come and then it will go. Just like the weather. The clouds will come and then the sun will shine and the clouds will come again. Your job is to see it, observe it, and let it come and let it go.

EXERCISE: STALKING THE MIND

If you have no awareness of what's moving through your mind, then you've probably become identified with your mind. You can only begin to dissolve this attachment if you are aware of the thoughts moving through, rather than identifying with the thoughts as truth. This stalking technique is the starting point for you to gain more awareness.

1. For one week, describe in your journal the thoughts and beliefs that repeatedly cross your mind. Think of it as stalking your mind. In particular, take notes around reactions, triggers, challenges and heightened emotion.

2. At the end of the week, review the notes and look for common threads. What is this showing you that has been living your life?

3. Write down any insights into where these repeated thoughts occur most frequently; what experiences and what emotions follow the thoughts? How does this affect the way in which you behave and show up in the world?

'BEING WITH' MEDITATION 2

Sit up straight, relaxed and comfortable, with your eyes closed. Breathe deeply and slowly.

Allow your body to meet yourself in the present.

For a period of 20 minutes, simply sit breathing and be the watcher of your own mind. Knowing it is not who you are. You have a mind but you are not a mind.

Try to see how the thoughts come and then go, like clouds in the sky. Watch them come, notice what they are, then watch them go. Notice who is watching these thoughts. And who is the one observing who is watching them?

Continue to watch and play with curiosity.

Describe in your journal any insights that you get from the meditation.

Feeling Our Emotions

One of the primary strategies we human beings use to deal with challenges is resistance. I'm a resister, or at least I was. When I look back on my addiction days, there were two main root causes for the way I was destroying my life. Firstly, I resisted everything to do with being present with what lay within me. Secondly, I simultaneously believed wholly and utterly that I was a worthless and unlovable person.

Both disconnected me from being in the present. Both kept me captive in the story. Neither gave me any peace; in fact, they created an enormous amount of suffering.

I can remember, when still only seven years old, already obsessing about what I was going to eat or not eat, how much I weighed, and how I could get boys to pay attention to me. At the age of 10, I was stealing cigarettes out of my sister's bag; by 11, stealing bottles of wine and downing them; at 13, consuming class A drugs as if they were my fuel. This behaviour spiralled progressively out of control, driven by an animalistic pull to escape my reality. It was a devastating existence. The desperation to escape consumed every part of my life, creating more and more suffering. In my attempt to avoid feeling pain, I created a life filled with endless suffering.

That is clear insanity, but we do it all the time, every day. And we call this our life and wonder why it's so tough. But the feelings aren't the issue – they're uncomfortable to experience, for sure, but they're not the cause of the problems. The problems are caused solely by our resistance to being with them as they rise in the present. Our resistance is a strategy to fix the pain, but that strategy will only get us back to where we were before, where nothing changes and the cause of the pain is still there. We may win a brief moment of 'feeling better', but not for long, and the wound will continue to fester.

Until we stop resisting and let ourselves feel. So it dissolves. And we heal.

For the first 10 years of my recovery I was never truly feeling my emotions. There was a lot of emotion happening – rivers and storms and waterfalls of emotion, to be honest. I was no longer running from my feelings with such destructive attempts to keep them at bay, but I was still getting caught up in a world of drama, chaos and suffering. This peace I'd heard others speak of certainly wasn't part of how I experienced life. I wasn't conscious of it at the time, but I wasn't feeling my emotions; I was 'felting' them.

There are two ways in which we experience feelings. There are those that arise in the body in the present moment, with the purpose of signalling to our mind significant information we need to know. These are signals that tell us clearly whether something feels right for us or wrong; that tell us whether someone is violating us or stepping out of line. Such signals tell us if we are on the right track for ourselves or whether we have gone out of alignment. This is feeling and it is extremely useful and valuable – an inbuilt guidance system that is completely reliable, but accessible only from within the present moment. When we feel

Feelings are like the weather.

Some days the sun will shine.

Then the clouds come, but
the sun will shine again.

~

emotions, not only do we benefit from this incredible guidance system but, as they also dissolve once felt fully, we don't need to carry the weight of them with us afterwards. This allows us to remain a clear, authentic and aligned channel in the here and now.

Then there are feltings: feelings attached to memories from the past in our minds. A reactivation and repetition of the past, occurring as if it is happening in the present. When we are felting, we are stuck in the past and we are stuck in the story (back in the well, like the frog). We're reliving the past on repeat here in the present. This detaches us from being in life, disconnecting us more and more from our truth and authenticity. Nothing dissolves when we are felting; we just go round and round on that hamster wheel, becoming more entrenched in the well. Sadly this is what most people are doing today, and this is what creates more problems and more patterns in which we get stuck.

As you read about these two distinct ways of experiencing emotion, take a moment to reflect for yourself: which one do you relate to? Scan through your day, your week, your life, and see. The surefire way to identify the distinction for yourself is this: one way will give you a sense of peace and freedom, aliveness and flow; the other will get you nowhere fast, with no reprieve and a whole load of suffering.

I was the latter.

Everything looked so much better than before. From the outside, my life had improved dramatically. My wallpaper was so pretty now. It looked like I was free. But I wasn't.

- Slim, healthy, pretty – check.

- Plant-based, clean, perfect eating – check.

- Nice flat in London – check.

- Handsome boyfriend – check.

- Back at school, training in my dream field (to do what I do now) – check.

- Not getting high, stealing, purging, lying or cheating – check.

My parents were overjoyed. I was finally fitting into the world they wanted for me. But behind closed doors I was still suffering. The feelings I'd struggled with when I got high were still there, I just wasn't getting high this time. Fear, insecurity, pain, worthlessness, shame, guilt, fear of abandonment, self-hatred, rage – all regularly reared their ugly head. My past was still living my present and living me. This wasn't what I'd signed up for. I wanted more.

To the Amazon I Go

So I packed my bags and took myself off on my first trip to the Amazon jungle, to work with plant medicine and to learn as much as I could from a shaman there. I knew I had absolutely nothing to lose. The moment I arrived, deep in the jungle, the shaman I'd committed to working with took one look and saw right through me. It was deeply unsettling. He instructed me to sit in complete silence for seven full days. What?!? No big, explosive, mind-altering experiences? No rainbow-coloured visions? To say I was disappointed was an understatement. But hey, I was there already so I did what he told me. During my period of silence I was not to leave my bed unless I needed to use the bathroom. Someone would bring me food twice a day and other than that I was to be still, in silence and complete solitude the entire time. Shit.

And so... I began.

For the first two days I could barely sit still. Fidgety and uncomfortable, moving around my bed as though I had ants crawling up and down my skin. By day three I felt like I was going mad. My mind was a constant stream of thoughts and judgements that I could not control or stop as I had nothing to distract myself with. Through my body erupted bursts of rage, then fear, then rage. I wanted so badly to run away, but I was alone deep in the middle of the Amazon – where would I go? When the shaman came to bring me food, I begged him (writing on paper, keeping my silence) to let me stop. It felt like too big a mountain for me to climb. He looked me straight in the eyes and said: 'This is to teach you how to be strong on the inside. To give you a solid foundation so you are not blown around in the storm like a leaf on the wind.'

His words pierced through me like shards of glass. He was right, but I hadn't even seen it until he said it. I'd felt like a leaf being blown around on the storm. Except the storm happened daily and the storm was my life. A stillness washed over me, and with it a courage I hadn't seen in a while. I wanted more. I wanted peace. I went back to my bed and continued. I surrendered the resistance. The next day something started to shift. My thoughts would come and go and come and go, but this time they weren't bothering me in any way. Just coming and going and coming and going as I'd watch them. None of it seemed to mean anything at all. They were just thoughts. I actually found it quite funny.

Then, on day five, something remarkable happened. Feelings would rise and then pass. With each rise I'd feel them so fully through every pore of my body; some painful, some uncomfortable, some euphoric.

But I simply let them rise and then pass, moving through my body like a wave, filling me completely, and then gone, like the tides ebbing and flowing on the shore. With every wave that rose through me, the walls around my heart began dissolving; those walls of protection I had carried forever, but hadn't even recognized until that moment. I felt it all while being present and grounded. The feelings were inside me but I was not inside the feelings. I sat there witnessing life moving in and out and in and out of me for the final few days. I'd never felt more alive, more at peace.

My whole life up to then had been a sequence of reactions to felting and thoughts in my mind. A life I'd not been present for at all, but I hadn't been able to see it until that moment on the bed.

For the first time in my entire life I felt free.

Dearest you. You do *not* need to fly off to the Amazon to learn this lesson. You don't need to go to the extremes I did. You can learn this lesson here and now – if you want to, and if you choose to. Emotions are energy moving through you. Feelings are inside you, but they are not you. To truly begin living beyond the story, aligned with who you are in this moment, is to be fully present with these experiences of life. All of it, unconditionally. To feel, without resistance, is to be present and alive with what is in the moment. Each day the tide will ebb and flow, and then ebb again. And with each passing wave that you allow to rise and fall within you, and you allow yourself to feel, the feeling dissolves and you heal. Life flows and sometimes it's uncomfortable – although there is always aliveness and some touch of beauty – but this is freedom.

EXERCISE: YOUR FEELINGS

1. What are the predominant emotional experiences that arise in your life? Do you have recurring emotions that have defined how you know yourself and how you experience life? Write down what they are in your journal.

2. In relation to the problems that you brought to this book, what are the repeated feelings that arise in these moments?

3. Write a few paragraphs to describe how much these feelings have shown up in your life: when, where, how. Do you allow yourself to actually feel them? Do you resist or submit?

4. List in your journal all the ways in which you resist or submit to feeling the emotions.

5. What do these emotions give you? For example: *attention, feeling of aliveness, feeling of power.* How much have you become attached and defined by them? Who would you be without them? Is there anyone in your past that you learned these emotional responses from? Do you want to surrender your attachment to these?

'OPENING YOUR HEART' MEDITATION

This meditation is very powerful when you are feeling stuck or blocked emotionally.

Sit comfortably, close your eyes and take three deep breaths, slowing right down. Meet yourself here.

Bring your awareness to your heart and place your hand here. Notice how your heart is. Is it hard or tense? Is it hurting, is it tender? Notice without judging. See what is there and say, 'I see you and you are welcome.'

Repeat this with all that you see, allowing yourself to really let in the acknowledgement.

Once all is acknowledged, start to deepen your in-breath so there is more energy bringing the breath to fill the heart. Expand the heart fully with the in-breath, and then exhale and let go.

Repeat again with a slow, vibrant, alive in-breath to fill the heart, allowing it to expand fully, and then exhale. Repeat this cycle for 3–4 more breaths as you bring more energy into your heart.

With your next in-breath, visualize the breath to be bright golden light, now expanding and filling your whole heart with its radiance. Then exhale and simply let go.

Continue this cycle for 3–4 more breaths, allowing your heart to be filled to the brim with this golden light vibration. As you inhale, visualize a tiny crack through the centre of your heart breaking open, with the most incredible bright golden light bursting through. Exhale and let go.

With every single in-breath bringing light into your heart, visualize the crack growing bigger, with more of this incredible, golden light bursting through like the sun. Continue until your whole heart is just an incredible golden sun burning bright, shining light fully out to the world from your heart.

Breathe here for as long as you feel your need, allowing the vibration to wash over you.

Slowly let your breath regulate once again. Gently open your eyes. Use your journal for any insights that came to you.

BODYWORK: SOMATIC DANCE PRACTICE

In TCM, feelings are energy or 'qi'. They come; they flow. When we become attached, they get stuck so cannot pass. This dance practice is a simple way to learn to be more with the feelings inside of you, rather than you being lost in the feelings. It can be particularly useful to practise this when you are feeling emotional in any way.

1. Close your eyes and take three deep breaths. Feel your feet rooted to the ground as you bring your awareness to centre.

2. Notice what emotions are within you right now: for example, anger, sadness, shame, guilt, fear, numbness. Notice where the emotion sits in your body. Notice what sensations it creates, what colour it is, what shape it is. Now, with your eyes closed, breathe deep, big, slow breaths and begin to allow your body to dance in whatever way it feels and needs with the emotion within you. You can of course play your own music to this practice and choose music to align with your emotional state.

3. Keep breathing deeply as you continue to dance with what is within you, allowing your awareness to drop deeper into the body and out of the mind, listening and learning how to move with this emotion. If it is sadness, do you need to flow like water? If it is anger, do you need to shake and stamp and shout? Notice how the emotion is inside of you, how it is an experience to dance with. But it is not you.

4. Continue this practice for 10 minutes if possible. Then slowly open your eyes. Write any insights you learn from this in your journal.

Commitment and Integration

Often, I'll tell a client there is ultimately nothing I'm going to do that will change their lives forever. I absolutely will offer an opening – a gateway, a possibility that may not have been there before – but the forever part? That's up to you. I'm not saying it to be mean (trust me, my ego wishes I could be the one that gets all the credit). But no matter how big an experience or 'aha!' moment you have, no matter how life-changing the shift in perception, I promise you that the euphoria will not last forever. Because ultimately you're still a human being with a mind and stories and feelings.

You may be able to ride the wave of the experience you had for quite some time, but if you really want to take that life-changing shift and turn it into your actual way of being in life then it all comes down to you. Maturation is not something we 'do' or 'find'. It is not a process of addition; it is a process of surrendering and letting go. It's about letting go of all that is not you in order for who you truly are to emerge. And remember, surrender is not a sign of weakness. It is not passive. It takes enormous courage and commitment to surrender strategies for survival and attachments to stories. It takes enormous commitment to continue surrendering every day for the rest of our lives.

When the frog popped his head over the top of the well it was an exhilarating and life-changing moment, but if he really wanted to make what he saw up there his actual life, he'd have to commit fully to taking every single step necessary to becoming free from the well. And with every step he'd mature a little bit more, and then a little bit more, until eventually he'd have grown so much that he outgrows the well and the world beyond it becomes integrated into his life.

After I returned from that first trip to the jungle, I knew that if I really wanted to take the peace and freedom I'd experienced there and turn it into my life, I was going to have to commit to a completely new relationship with my mind, my feelings, myself and my life, every single day. I was reminded of a time when I'd flown home and had to deal with not just a chaotic airport but also a break-up with my then boyfriend at home, and I'd felt all the usual emotions: abandonment, unworthiness, rejection. I saw clearly that moments such as that were going to happen again and again, and each time was an opportunity for me to respond to it differently. This new way of being would require a continued surrender and commitment. Even twenty minutes before I sat down to write this section of the book, the thoughts running through my head were: *Who am I to write this book? You're all going to laugh at me. I'm not good enough.* Every single day requires a surrender of the story and a commitment to show up anyway. And now the chapter written, and I'm still here.

This is the path we are on: not the path of feeling better and devoid of our humanness, but the path of being our full selves – humanness and all – while becoming free.

To surrender who you think you are, in order to allow who you were born to be to emerge, is a choice that you'll be invited to make every

If we do not integrate,

we do not change.

~

single day, and it's an act of courage and love. Surrendering the pull to survive in order to adopt a commitment to freedom, authenticity and truth is an act of courage and love. It's a life-long commitment that has nothing to do with getting it right or being perfect or not messing up. It has nothing to do with not getting triggered again or not being pulled back into the well. It's about being free.

You absolutely *will* be pulled back into your well. You absolutely *will* get triggered. You absolutely *will* have times when beliefs and memory and programming of your mind and from the past come back to contaminate how you see and experience the world and your life. Making this commitment doesn't mean none of these things will happen ever again. Expect them to happen again. This is about how you are willing to respond when they do happen.

Every time you're able to feel in the present moment and let something pass, you mature a little bit. Every time you see more clearly with consciousness and non-attachment, you mature a little bit more. And every time you're able to let the thoughts come and go without identifying with them, you mature a little bit more. Until you wake up one morning and you've matured so much that you're more *you* than you've ever been in your life. Something old has dissolved and you have evolved.

And that is how this goes. That is what it takes to really heal and that is what it takes to be free.

So many people want the big, sensational experiences, such as the fun one-night stand, then end up kicking and screaming their way through the long haul that is the actual integration process – the marriage. But it is only in the marriage that the true magic happens. The marriage is the part where you build a life.

And it's like coming home. Which it is, exactly: coming home.

Even Zen masters teach: 'After you have reached vast caverns of great expansion, eventually, someone needs to make the coffee.'

EXERCISE: COMMITMENT

1. Ask yourself: what is your relationship to commitment? Do you have an expectation of a quick fix? What comes up for you around committing to a way of living every day for the rest of your life?

2. Here and now, are you willing to make the commitment to this process for the long term? A commitment to yourself for yourself and for your life?

PHASE 2

Love

Love can be soft and tender or

a lioness killing for her cubs.

Love is not what we do, it's

why we do what we do.

Love is a space to come from.

Love is who you are.

~

CHAPTER 4

What Are You Making It Mean?

'The most difficult times for many of us are the ones we give ourselves.'

PEMA CHÖDRÖN

At the beginning of my separation, I had a profound seeing of something I'd never been able to see before. By then, I'd been living for a month as a single mother with my two young kids and it wasn't easy. I was up most nights with a teething baby, and supporting a six-year-old daughter who was struggling emotionally with the fact that her father had left. Plus I was running my business, seeing clients, writing this book and somehow trying to find time to take care of my own heart, which was utterly broken. But then I had a profound seeing.

On one particular day, I noticed as soon as I woke that everything felt harder than ever. Making the kids' breakfast felt hard, the baby's screaming felt hard, getting my daughter to school: hard. Showing up for work, showing up for life: just so hard.

The next morning (literally the next day), I noticed as soon as I woke up that everything felt easy. As I had breakfast with the kids there was ease and play and joy. When the baby cried, I felt peaceful and accepting. On the way to school my daughter and I skipped and laughed and played. I even noticed the birds singing and the flowers blooming. The whole day just felt peaceful, at ease, as if I was in the flow.

Observing the difference in these two back-to-back days was pretty amazing to me.

How could two days be experienced so differently, when nothing on the outside had changed at all? Things were still tough, yet how I felt about things was so different. There was only one aspect that had changed between day one and day two, yet it was so significant that it allowed me to feel as though I was living two different lives.

And here's what was different: whether I was making everything mean something or whether I wasn't.

On the hard day, my mind was having a field day, full of self-judgement and berating and self-shaming, every word of which I believed. When the baby cried, I heard: *Oh you're such a crap mom and the baby doesn't even like you.* Making breakfast, I heard: *I'm so alone, I'm going to be alone forever and it's because I'm a failure and nobody will love me.* Getting my daughter to school: *Life is so hard and it's because I'm worthless; I couldn't even keep my family together.* On and on, all day long.

On the easy day, that narrative may have still been going on but I had no attachment to it at all. I didn't make all my outside circumstances mean so much, and with that came the ability to be in the flow with life as it was, without anything needing to change. Freedom and peace.

We get taught from day one that if we can just find that something 'out there' with all the answers, it'll bring us peace, happiness and wholeness. This narrative merely affirms the story that who we are and where we are, as we are, is just not good enough. But if that's true, why can I have two days that appear completely identical from the outside and yet have two completely opposite experiences of them from the inside?

It's not what we are doing, or what we have, or what we get, that determines our ability to be at peace and in the flow with life. That is determined by what we're making it mean about who we are: whether we're making it mean everything.

Yes, if you're separated and living alone with the kids, it's very hard and it's very painful. This is true. But it doesn't need to mean that you're a failure and you'll be alone forever.

Yes, if you've binged again and are falling asleep with a stomach and heart that hurts, it's sad and it's painful and it's not where you wish to be. But it doesn't need to mean you're unworthy and unlovable.

Our life experiences and the behaviour patterns in which we find ourselves stuck do mean something. But they do not need to mean everything. Think about it for a moment. Look at something you find challenging in your life right now: maybe it's your job or your marriage; maybe it's your weight or your eating habits. I invite you to reflect. Is it really the 'thing' that is causing all the suffering? Or is the suffering actually caused more by the meaning you're giving the 'thing'; by what you are making it mean about you and your life? When I had the bad day and my baby was crying over breakfast, was I suffering because he was crying? Or was I suffering because I made his crying mean that I was a failure?

The narrative in your mind is memory from the past, inherited wholly and entirely from everyone and everywhere else. The narrative is not aligned with what is present in the moment. Attachment to the narrative immediately transports you back into your story.

If you really want to live beyond the story and free yourself from the well, it will require you to stop making everything mean everything about who you are. It will require you to surrender. And when you can and if you do, all the drama and chaos that was there before will dissolve.

This is step one, my dear friend. Maybe everything doesn't mean something. Maybe it just is what it is, for now

Paul's Story

When Paul first came to me, he was working hard to change his future by going back to school to become an acupuncturist. He was also a recovering alcoholic.

The story he was captive in was that he was a 'screw-up', a 'failure'. During his alcoholism he had hurt many people, but he'd hurt himself more than he'd hurt anyone else. In his recovery he had to learn from scratch how to show up for himself in a brand-new way. When we began our process together, he was coming to the end of his training and was in the middle of completing his dissertation. Showing up every day for class was exhilarating and challenging in equal measure. He was terrified that he'd get so pulled back into his story that he'd sabotage his exams and therefore his dreams.

These were the questions at the root of his fears: who would he be if he graduated? Was he even allowed to have such good things in his life? What if he delivered the paper and still failed massively? Maybe it would be best to just not hand it in at all? Paul was scared of staying stuck in the story, and scared of who he would be without it.

As the deadline loomed closer, it was becoming harder and harder for Paul to actually show up and continue writing. Although he was getting closer to changing the story for himself, the nature of a story (the mind) is to fight to survive. Yet Paul committed fully to the process, he kept putting one foot in front of the other, and he just kept writing.

Then, 24 hours before he needed to hand in the final piece of work, holed up at home, writing non-stop to get it done, he started to feel very uncomfortable. Before he knew it, he'd got up from his desk, walked into the kitchen and drunk an entire bottle of red wine that belonged to his flatmate. And now he was hammered.

Paul wasn't sure how it had even happened and he started to panic. Just like that, his past had hijacked him – he was back in the well.

But this time he responded to the situation very differently. Instead of spiralling into a pit of drama and chaos and making it all mean everything about who he is and who he isn't, he called me and I said to him: 'Clearly not the best behaviour. And it's because your story got the better of you. We know that to be truth. But that is the only truth that we know. Yes, it does mean something, which we will look at another time. But for now, it does not need to mean everything. Drink as much water as you can, sit on the sofa, and watch TV until you sober up. As soon as you do, get back to your writing until it's finished. Then show up at submission and hand it in on time. No drama. No chaos. Just keep putting one foot in front of the other. Okay?'

And that is exactly what he did. He sobered up by midnight, wrote all night, showed up at his college submission one hour before the deadline and handed in his dissertation.

He made a commitment not to make what had happened mean everything, yet he was absolutely determined to learn as much from it as he could.

Paul graduated and has not had a drink again since that night. He has also continued to carve out a whole new life for himself.

Paul's story could have turned out very differently, as it can for any of us in any moment on any day. He could have used that moment as the evidence he needed to prove that the story about himself as 'the failure' was true, and then to use that evidence as a reason to bail on himself and his dreams. He could have made it mean everything, which would have left him with nothing.

Or at least no possibility for peace, freedom or change.

You are no different to Paul. Because you are a human being. And as a human being, you will get triggered and – for a while at least – there is a risk that you will be pulled back into your story. So when this happens, and you're able to commit to choosing freedom over suffering, you're making the first step towards change.

Do not make it mean *everything*. Keep moving forwards: one foot in front of the other, one step at a time. Your peace and happiness are not determined by what you do or what you achieve or where you go. Happiness is a habit. A habit of being at peace with 'what is' in the present moment.

Surrender the suffering and just keep walking.

EXERCISE: ATTACHING MEANING

1. What problem led you to pick up this book? Write a paragraph or two in your journal, describing what you have made this problem mean about you?

2. As honestly as you can, write down five examples of really challenging days. For each example, include details of what problem was happening *and* what you were making it mean about you or your life.

3. Now list the consequences that unfolded each time as a result of the meaning you attached to it.

4. Reflection: was it the 'problem' that caused the suffering, or was it the narrative you attached to that problem?

5. Does the meaning you put on things support the story you've been identified with, as evidence to prove it right?

6. How differently could things have unfolded in all five experiences if you hadn't given them the meaning you did? How could that have changed your life?

7. Are you willing to surrender the meaning to let yourself *be with* the experience and the unknown quality that comes with it?

Bye-bye Victimhood

One of the most common questions I get asked is: 'How did you end up teaching and leading maturation?' My answer is always this: 'I never looked for it; I wasn't trying to find this – in fact, the opposite occurred: it found me. What I did was dedicate myself to the path of my own healing, and the more I surrender what is not me or mine or true to my authenticity, the more I come home to who I was born to be. And my path – this purpose of mine – well, it found me.'

Our maturation isn't something we need to do or find; there's nothing magical about it. It's already within each and every one of us as part of our essential nature. Some teachers have even described it as our destiny as human beings, which I believe to be true. Whether it takes one lifetime or many lifetimes, the calling is there already within each one of us to remember who we are and to come home to our authentic truth. The more we surrender the story – the narrative, the survival – the more we can hear our calling and let it lead us home.

As human beings we're destined to grow. No matter how much we try to stop it, avoid it or escape it, our physical bodies will keep growing and keep maturing. That's a given. The same is true of our emotional, mental, spiritual self. It's part of our essential nature – it's part of our destiny – to keep maturing; like the seed's destiny is to become a tree or the caterpillar's destiny is to become a butterfly. It is in our essential nature to mature in all areas: mind, body, emotions, heart, soul, spirit.

To continue on our path of maturation on any level other than physical, however, we need to be present in life. We need to be living rather than surviving. The moment we vacate living and start surviving, our maturation process stops. We become frozen in time, stuck in the past, detached from the present, disconnected from life. And the mental, emotional, spiritual age in which we are frozen is the age at which we began identifying with the story; that's the age at which we forgot who we truly are.

Until we begin the process of surrender.

The moment we are ready to surrender ourselves out of what we know is the moment we return to our maturation process. With every moment of surrender, the story dissolves a little more and we return more to authentic alignment; to who we were always born to be. And the only one who can allow the process to happen is you. You're going to need to surrender up the victim behind your story in order to mature into your full, whole, empowered adult self.

Finally Growing Up

Six months after returning from my first trip to Peru, I was deep in the process of my integration. My head had popped over the top of the well, but now the real work had begun – the continuous commitment and surrendering in order to allow the gifts I gained to become my life.

Coming to the end of my second year of training to be an Integrative Counsellor, I found myself acting out in destructive ways again. Basically I was totally fucking it up. Coming out of a volatile relationship and caught up in the drama – wanting him, not wanting him, wanting him, not wanting him – I started missing modules at school and not doing my homework. As I got closer and closer to my final exams, the prospect of me failing was very real, as I hadn't done any revision. I was on a fast track to repeating the same old story I'd always been in ('I am bad'), but this time I had enough awareness to watch myself doing it, even though I didn't know how to stop it.

I started to panic, so I went to my teacher, told him what I was doing and asked for help. These were his words to me: 'Nicky, who are you going to have to forgive or what do you need to surrender, in order to allow yourself to become an empowered, fulfilled, joyful woman? As long as you are blaming the people from your past, blaming yourself, blaming the world for how you are, you will forever stay the wounded child. The moment you are willing to surrender the victim and become fully accountable for your life, you will allow yourself to become the woman you were born to be.'

I honestly didn't know whether I wanted to hug him or throw my chair at him.

But I heard him. I heard him loud and clear.

As I took the time to reflect on those questions he'd asked me, I felt a deep pain, followed by rage. The pain came from recognition that there was nothing I was ever going to be able to do that would change my past. No matter how much I tried, I couldn't go back in time to change what had happened for me, and this was a devastating moment of insight: my past was gone and I'd never fully grieved it or let it go. I'd been trying to live in a way that could somehow make it different; I'd been in survival. But if I wanted a future beyond the past, I'd have to be the one now to show up for me, wholly self-responsible – no more blaming, no more victimhood. A strange mix of devastating grief and unbelievable love moved through me: pain and beauty, breaking and opening, surrendering and coming home, all at once. I knew I was still holding on to so much resentment towards my mother, my father and even myself, in an attempt to control what had happened and mask the pain. Finally, however, something broke; I surrendered that last grip I had left on my narrative of the past and it felt as though my heart broke into a million pieces.

Finally, I was able to see clearly that all the blame and resentment within me was keeping me bound in a state of holding on, and it was keeping me stuck as the victimized child. I knew then that it was time to let go and to forgive.

The vibrational field of victimhood is the same as that of survival; there is simply no power there. More victimhood means more survival, and the deeper we feel it, the more we block our own empowerment and stay stuck in the past. Being victimized is what happened to us; living in victimhood is how we identify with what happened to us. The first we cannot always prevent or control; the second is on us and is our responsibility. As long as someone 'out there' or something 'out there' is to blame, as long as we hold on to hate and resentment, we are giving our power away to others and rejecting it for ourselves. And we are feeding ourselves and our lives with the same vibrational field in which we received our pain. Nothing can heal in this environment; nothing can grow or change.

We cannot control life. It can be very random sometimes, and challenges happen that are inexplicable and painful. What we can control is our response to life, and it is in responding to life rather than reacting that we consciously create from a place beyond survival and beyond story. Do we use the challenges as a way to go deeper into the story or do we use them to deliver us to a place beyond the story? This is a choice you're going to have to make repeatedly as you surrender more, and a choice to make continuously throughout the rest of your life.

I saw how attached I was to being the victim, but now I was ready to take back my power and make peace with all those I was blaming for my pain and my suffering.

I wrote letters to both my mother and father, thanking them for the gifts that they had given me throughout my life. I made amends to them for the anger and blame I'd been holding on to all this time, and I consciously took full responsibility for who I am now, for what I needed, and for the kind of life I truly dreamt of.

I also wrote a letter to myself, making amends for the years of self-abandonment, self-berating, self-judgement and sabotage. I made a commitment to show up for myself from that point forwards as the mother and father I'd always longed for. I cried and grieved and laughed and cried some more.

I was amazed at the power of sending those letters. The moment I'd posted them, a huge weight lifted from my shoulders and more walls around my heart dissolved. The letters were part of it, of course, but the real shift had happened inside me, through the choice and commitment I'd made and in the surrendering of the victim story. I'd let a wall crumble and, as I stood there surrounded by rubble, it was as though a huge gateway had opened up that I hadn't even known was there, and I could feel that I'd set them free too.

My darling father is not the best of dads but, God, he is a wonderful human being. When I let go of resenting all the things he hadn't given me, I started to see all the gifts he had. From him I inherited this incredible desire to be fully alive, and his amazing ability to make those around him feel loved and seen and important. For the first time in my life I truly acknowledged how much I carried him in my pores and it was a gift.

My darling mother has suffered almost all of her life and, when I let go of the blame I'd placed on her, I started to see how similar we are. Underneath the fight, underneath the behaviour, was a broken heart. As I became able to be more available for healing my own heart, I was able to be more available for hers too. And the gifts she has given me. My God, that woman can rise from the ashes through the toughest of life experiences and I know I've inherited this fire, this courage, this passion from her. Her spirit is that of a phoenix rising, and that spirit is alive and profoundly powerful in me today, for which I'm forever grateful. For the first time in my life, I settled deeper into the pores of my being as I welcomed the lineage from which I'd come.

I went on to do very well in my training, passing with flying colours and graduating with distinction. I can say wholeheartedly that I am the empowered, fulfilled, joyful woman I once dreamt of becoming. The moment we surrender and become committed to being fully accountable, all the energy we formerly expended on keeping us stuck in victimhood is released, like a river no longer held back by a dam, and we get to be nourished and fed and replenished by all that life again. Life can be expressed more fully and wholly and alive through us and from us in a way that creates more life.

EXERCISE: BLAME

1. Who do you blame or consider responsible for the story that is keeping you in victimhood? Write a few paragraphs in your journal about who it is and why you are holding on to this.

2. As you write the paragraphs above, notice any experiences or feelings moving through your body. Can you notice the energy and charge held captive in the blaming?

3. Do you notice yourself blaming others in your life in a similar way: partners, children, yourself, teachers? Are there any repeated patterns with this behaviour and when it occurs? How much does this keep you in the victim role? Capture your observations in your journal.

4. At what other times in your life do you end up as the victim? What happens, how and why? Is this who you want to continue being? Can you see how much this behaviour keeps you even more in survival? Are you willing to surrender this?

Boundaries Are Love

Committing to living beyond victimhood can only become possible with boundaries. Like the fence between neighbours that allows a mutually happy and respectful relationship, boundaries are lines between what is me and what is you; what is mine and what is yours. Boundaries create a safe space for ourselves and a clear sense of our own truth. Without boundaries we lose these necessary lines, losing ourselves in each other and abandoning ourselves for each other; creating an environment that is unsafe, breeding self-abandonment and resentment, and keeping us in victimhood – and back in survival.

When I look at my childhood, I can see that my father leaving, or being on the receiving end of my mother's rage, were not the factors that had the greatest impact on my sense of self – even though these things had a significant impact on how I came to know myself in the world. What had an even greater impact was witnessing my mother continually abandon herself. As big as her heart is, and as great as her efforts were to do the best for us she could, what I witnessed was devastating: she would continually lose herself over and over again to other people's wants and needs, and lacked any care for her own wellbeing and health. I never saw her do anything that was an action for her own self or truth during those early years, and that became normal to me. I learned from her that to be good, to be unselfish and to love meant to give up everything about yourself in order to please others. It took me a very long time to learn that this is not love. This is fear. This is co-dependency, and this is not healthy. At the core of this behaviour is the message: 'My value and worth is so little that I will abandon who I am in order to please you.' This is what I learned about myself and this is what I brought into my own life.

As I grew up through my teenage years and into womanhood, I had no idea what boundaries were. I had no idea that I could say no when things didn't feel right, or turn down invitations when I didn't want to go. I had no idea that it was allowed for me to put my needs and desires and wellbeing at the forefront of my life. I was so identified with being worthless and of no value. This is who I believed I was, and in support of this I'd do anything to make sure people loved me. Throughout my addiction years, there were countless times I gave my body to men I didn't like, just to receive anything that would affirm my value and worth. I spent years changing myself to fit friends' values and beliefs, moulding myself to please my parents and everyone I ever met.

By the time I was in recovery, I had no idea who I was or what my own values were. I had no sense of self; no voice of my own. It was a desperately painful way to exist. Every time I failed to honour my own truth, I disconnected a little more from my sense of self, feeding the disconnection created by my childhood trauma and allowing my story to live my life.

This was not living.

Boundaries are not just a good thing to have. They are the very lines that allow us to distinguish between what is you and what is me; the lines that allow me to be me safely and you to be you safely. They delineate the space that we can inhabit as who we authentically are, with a clear sense of ourselves – a sense of our worth, value, truth – and a connection to a deeper knowing that is within every one of us.

You are allowed to be you, all of you, the whole of you. And I'm allowed to be me, all of me, the whole of me.

Living with good boundaries is owning responsibility for what is our truth and not getting entangled in someone else's. Boundaries create safety, trust and a strong foundation to be able to love more. When I think of all the people I feel most safe with, they are the ones that have really good boundaries. They say what they feel, say when they don't want to do things and when they have had enough, and they take full responsibility for themselves. They speak truth in honour of themselves and I can trust them.

Being 'nice' is not the same as 'love'. Being 'nice' is a way of presenting ourselves that is taught as 'good'. But often being 'nice' is the presentation of a character that plays 'niceness' without honouring what is real and true beneath the surface. Being 'nice' is the same as 'feeling better'; like putting 'nice' wallpaper up. It looks good, but soon you will realize you are trapped in this character and you are not free. Boundaries allow us to acknowledge what is true for ourselves and we can choose to listen and honour this, prioritizing it over needing to be 'nice' or needing to please others. Boundaries allow us to choose authenticity and aliveness over presentation and survival. Boundaries are the active part of listening and seeing more clearly. Having boundaries is saying: 'What is true for me is important to me right now.'

Adult to Adult

During the early days of recovery, learning to set boundaries in honour of my needs and truth was like learning how to walk for the first time. It was so unfamiliar to me but an absolutely necessary part of healing. I had to learn how to stand on my own two feet and in my own truth if I was ever to have any chance of living free. At first, I had to start with really small things, which at the time still felt like climbing a mountain. 'I'm not hungry right now so I'll eat later.' 'Thank you but I don't feel like coming out tonight; I need a quiet night to myself.' 'Thank you but I don't wish to see you again.' (That was after a terrible first date!)

An absolute revelation. I didn't even know I was allowed to listen and behave in honour of what was true for me, whether or not someone else didn't like it or didn't agree. It was certainly uncomfortable being on the receiving end of others' disappointment and difficult feelings in response to my new behaviour, but I committed to letting others have their experience while I let myself have mine. Learning that it's okay for people to feel pain, disappointment, and anger, as part of what they need to feel and experience in their own truth. And learning that I don't have to turn myself inside out to stop others from feeling these emotions at the expense of my truth. The more I honoured me, the more I honoured you. With every boundary I set, I found myself feeling safer in myself. A safety I'd never felt before. I learned that I could be someone I could actually trust and the more I trusted myself, the more I was able to make choices in my life that honoured who I am. And as I got more confident, the boundaries got braver.

Five years into recovery, I was living in New York and working in a restaurant when my father came to visit me. He came to eat at the restaurant but, while I was waiting tables, I heard a commotion in the area in which he was sitting. He had got drunk and was having a loud argument with my stepmother. Everyone in the restaurant turned around to look and, after a stern look from my manager, I had to walk him out of the restaurant, stumbling all over the place, and get him into a cab back to his hotel. I was mortified. When he came to see me the next day, he was desperately sorry. But instead of doing what I'd normally do, which was smile sweetly and be his good, adoring girl, I looked him straight in the eye and said, 'I love you, but your behaviour last night was unacceptable to me. It left me feeling embarrassed and really unsafe. I am hurt and angry with you right now.'

I had never spoken like that to him ever in my life. As I spoke, I realized that the voice coming out of my mouth sounded not like a little girl but like a woman, and because I spoke to him as an adult, in a grounded and loving way, he heard me. That moment was the point at which my relationship with my father changed for the better in every way. He began respecting me and treating me like an adult woman, and I felt safer with him because I trusted myself to put boundaries down and take care of myself. The more responsible I was for my own sense of truth, the less resentful I became and the more love I had to give. And the more comfortable I was to use my voice, share myself, and be myself – less victim, more woman. I was freeing myself more and more from the well.

Boundaries are the lines that allow you to discover and own your authenticity, and the more authentically you can be in your life, the more aligned the life you create will be with your truth. Boundaries are an act of love, for everyone involved, even when they don't always feel that way.

As you emerge more and more from the confines of your story, you will have to begin to set some bigger boundaries. Ones that are staking your claim to your own authenticity and freedom. And when you do that, you are making living free the main priority in life – and that is incredibly empowering.

EXERCISE: FINDING YOUR BOUNDARIES

1. In your journal, describe five situations recently when you didn't say what you really meant or felt in order to please another. How did this leave you feeling? What impact does it have on your worth, energy, heart and health? What impact does it have on your relationships?

2. Write a few paragraphs about how not setting boundaries keeps you in victimhood. Is this who you really want to be?

3. Write down three examples of situations in your life right now in which you need to use your voice or set a boundary, in order to be responsible for yourself and not end up the victim again. How can you do it? What do you need to say? How does it feel in your body as you think about doing it? Are you ready to commit to this?

4. Note in your journal any insights you have *after* you've had those three conversations.

Compassion: the Gateway to the Heart

My teacher David has led maturation programmes all over the world for almost 50 years. He's led programmes in North America, many parts of Western Europe, Australia, India and Israel. He often observes that however different we all are, beneath all the differences – of which there are many – we are also all the same. The sameness has to do with the design of being human. We struggle with the same pains and have the same needs. And although our survival strategies may be different, the fact that we live in survival is the same. When he shared this with me, I found it remarkable and yet something that felt so right and true. It was like remembering something I've always known.

We focus so much on the outside layers of how to see each other, defining each other based on what we see, and we do the same to ourselves. But if we're willing to look much deeper, beneath the surface, we'll see that we are all the same. This is such a fundamental life learning. It's only when we're willing and able to see ourselves in each other, and offer understanding and compassion, that we can begin to live beyond the realms of blame, judgements, separation and victimhood.

The definition of compassion is to see the struggle beneath the behaviour of another and of ourselves and to give allowance and understanding to that struggle and pain. We may not yet be able and ready to give it love, but we can give it understanding. This understanding is what allows the fight and judgement and blaming to be released, and allows the punishing attachment to survival and victimhood to dissolve. To be able to truly see ourselves and others beyond behaviour and stories is a gift of maturity and a step to freedom. To see and know that behaviour is a survival strategy and beneath it is a human being with a deep wound of pain and heartbreak offers a level of freedom, love, openness and aliveness that we can't access when we are trapped in the realms of separation.

First and foremost, compassion needs to begin with you and for you.

Who you are is not your story, nor is it the struggles you have and what you have been through in your life. Nor are you defined by your behaviour or your patterns, thoughts, feelings, mistakes and fears.

These are what you have identified with, and strategies you have used to survive, but they are not who you are. When you can begin bringing compassion to yourself and to the humanity within you, and give yourself the seeing and acknowledgement that you so need and deserve, this will open up such a deep and beautiful pathway to your healing process.

You cannot be the victim while being a space of love and honour for yourself too. Take a moment to scan through your life, scan through the behaviours and patterns and stories, and allow yourself to drop deeper and see beneath it all. Beneath, there has been a deep need you have and a pain that you've found difficult to feel. If you can allow yourself to even see it, beneath the surface, and offer some understanding and compassion, you're ready to heal on a very deep level. When you begin to see yourself in this way, you can begin to see the possibility of who you are beyond the story, opening a doorway you may not have seen before.

Clara's Story

My client Clara lived through one of the most devastating childhoods of anyone I've ever known or worked with. To survive, she had of course created a story: she needed to be hyper-vigilant and in control of every detail in her life. Tough, hardened, protective, she would move, speak and think at such a fast pace that in our first session she was almost vibrating in the chair in front of me. Everything about the way Clara existed in the world was about making sure she was going to be safe. Of course it was.

Sadly, the impact this was having on her life was heartbreaking. She struggled to have any close friends and would push away anyone who tried to get to know her and love her. She struggled in love relationships and found it impossible to trust, always on the lookout for evidence that she should run and push people away. Her whole life had become a well of survival and she had no idea how to get out. Worst of all was how she punished herself for being how she was: in a constant war with herself for not being able to trust, not being able to let love in, not being able to allow any other way. And the more she punished herself, the more unsafe she felt, and the deeper into her story she was.

The first part of our process together was focused on learning to bring compassion to herself, to surrender the fight and survival in order to begin feeling and to face the pain she carried within her from her past. And to see, beneath the behaviour, the terrified little girl in pain. What she needed more than anything was to feel safe and loved and held and seen, not punished.

After some time, she was able to see more clearly the story she was stuck in. She saw that by berating herself so harshly, she was continuing the abuse of her past and bringing it into her present. With every moment in which she was able to give herself compassion instead of punishment, the walls of her story began dissolving and she began healing, discovering a new sense of safety, love and holding for herself that she had never known before. Slowly, step by step, one act of compassion and awareness at a time, she began to surrender more and more of the survival, meeting herself in more authenticity each time.

We then started looking at her parents. If she truly wanted to become free of the story, we needed to look at what she was still holding on to that was keeping her entrenched in victimhood, and look at the anger, rage and blame she was still carrying towards them both.

And so I gave her homework to go away and do: to write the detailed life stories of her parents and to read them aloud to me in our next session. It was important she didn't write about them as 'Mum' or 'Dad' but as individuals, with names, lives, and feelings of their own.

As she read it out, we would stop regularly to allow her to connect with what each parent might have been feeling and experiencing at a particular time in their lives. Each time she allowed herself to connect with what that human being was living through and experiencing, something would shift within her. For the first time in her life, she was able to see them both as human beings, with their own feelings, needs, stories and struggles. She could even empathize with the pain both carried within them that led them to behave as they did.

Clara recognized clearly that they had both behaved in ways that were hurtful, but now she had some insight and understanding as to why – not just on a conceptual level, but on a deep experiential level within her heart. More importantly, she saw that their behaviour had nothing to do with her. They behaved the way they did because of their own pain; their own stories. For the first time ever, Clara saw that there was nothing wrong with her and that she had always been worthy of love. Bringing compassion to her parents allowed Clara to have a deeper compassion for herself and, in fact, a deeper compassion for all human beings, opening her heart in a way she had never experienced before.

None of this could ever take the pain away or change the past, but it allowed her to surrender the victimhood and become more accountable for herself in every way. Today, Clara is a powerful coach, holding space for people's struggles and pain, and teaching them how to know their own freedom and peace. The compassion she holds in her own heart only expands her ability to connect with other humans in a much deeper, authentic way.

Being able to see beyond someone's behaviour and story is not only an act of love towards them, it is an act of love for ourselves. Every moment of compassion we bring to ourselves, we bring to another, and vice versa. Compassion lessens the distances and separation between us. It creates wholeness, teaching us and reminding us that we are all connected; that on the surface no two people are the same, yet at the deepest level we are all the same. It reminds us that we are not and never have been alone; that who we are is not what we do. Beneath the layers of strategy and protections we have built for ourselves, there is a whole being that has needs for love, connection, fulfilment, community and truth.

This applies to everyone. And it applies to you.

The more you can begin to see yourself and others in this way, the more you will heal. And the more the story will no longer fit, like a costume you've grown out of. See yourself and others as a whole being, distinct from behaviour and story, and the trajectory of your healing will soar.

EXERCISE: WRITE A LIFE STORY

1. I know this is a biggie. Choose one of the people you are blaming the most for the story you are in and for the problems and struggles in your life. For this particular exercise this person *cannot* be you. Write their life story, from the day they were born to as far as you can go. Call them by their first name, take them out of the role in which you know them. What did they live through? What would it have felt like? What were they struggling with? Go deep into their story.

2. When you have finished, I want you to read the story out to somebody else or to yourself. Read slowly and consciously. Every now and then, pause to let what they were feeling and going through really enter into your heart. What can you see? What have you learned?

3. What do you not forgive yourself for? What are you holding on to? Write it all down as honestly as you can.

4. Now go through each issue and write what was going on beneath the behaviour. What did you need? What were you struggling with? What were you trying to survive? Can you offer yourself compassion?

5. Write yourself a letter to make amends for all the times you've been hard on yourself and to forgive yourself for all the times you've blamed yourself. Once you finish writing the letter, I invite you to put it in an envelope with a stamp and your address on the front, and to post it the moment you finish reading this book!

'COMPASSION' MEDITATION

Sit comfortably and take three deep breaths, slowly bringing your awareness inwards.

Now I want you to become really present to one of the things for which you're blaming yourself so badly. Bring a memory of a time when you were acting out in this behaviour. Really see yourself there and allow the feelings of that memory and experience to move through you.

As you look at yourself in this memory, look deep into your heart. How young are you? Are you a child? Of what age?

What was it that you really needed and were trying to gain in this memory? Did you know how to do it any other way? Can you see that you had deeper needs within you and were doing the best you could?

Now look over at yourself and send yourself so much compassion for going through what you went through. Fill yourself with compassion and take a few more deep breaths.

Now I want you to become really present to the person you have been blaming the most. Bring a memory of a time when they were really acting out in the way for which you blame them. Allow the feelings of that memory to move through you.

Now look over at them and look deep within them. How old are they really in this memory? Or how young are they really? What are you really feeling and needing inside?

Is this survival behaviour all they know?

See them. Can you send them compassion too?

Breathe and fill yourself with compassion as you send it to them until it fills them up and fills you up.

When you are ready, bring your breath back to the present, regulate your breathing, and slowly open your eyes.

Use your journal to write any insights or 'aha!' moments from this meditation.

CHAPTER 5
Coming Out of Hiding

'Out beyond ideas of wrongdoing and rightdoing there is a field. I'll meet you there.'

RUMI

I want to ask you a really important question: who would you wish to be if you were to live beyond your story? Close your eyes and ask yourself: *How would it feel being me if I were not trying to survive my past?* Allow yourself to let this question into your entire being, not as a question that needs to be answered, but a question that can be heard and received and lived.

Notice, I asked you who would you wish to be. I didn't ask how you'd want your life to look or how you wished to look. One of the greatest sources of fuel for our story is the idea that one day we might reach the end of the search and find the prize dangling there: the beautiful happy ending that will rescue us from the devastation of our own emptiness and unworthiness. Somewhere out there one day. We hold pictures in our mind of where that 'somewhere' could be, believing that if we finally 'get there', the struggle will be over and we'll be free. That fantasy far off in the distance that if we could just do the right things, or find the right ways, or be better than we are right now, we will finally 'get there' and we will be whole and happy and at peace.

But sadly, it is one of the greatest illusions of all. The problem with fantasies is that they are always somewhere-out-there-one-day, but they are never here and they are never now. Like a dangled carrot, the fantasy will keep us in a state of perpetual striving, always seeking and searching for the next thing that will get us out of where we are now. These pictures in our fantasy are birthed by the character we've been in the story, needing to survive. Part of the story of who we thought we were, and who we told ourselves we needed to be, to overcompensate for who we believe we are ('I'm not worthy', for example, or 'I'm bad').

But here's the problem with pictures: pictures are not real. They're static images in the mind made up of conditioning, beliefs and assumptions that are based on memories from the past. We're so focused on 'out there', trying to strive for the pictures, that we're missing the actual living of life here and now. A picture will never give us what we truly want. A picture can only offer us a certain way to *look*, but it has nothing to do with how we wish to feel, how we wish to be living, or who we wish to be. What we really want to know is how we wish to *feel* being ourselves, sitting in our own skin in our own lives; here in the present, alive, connected.

Our freedom only exists in the here and now. There is no freedom in a picture. Letting go of pictures is letting go of control and letting go of the need to survive. It is a deep surrender, letting go of the fantasy of knowing how it is all going to turn out, and of the longing and hoping for a happy ending – one that will rescue us from the realities of who we actually are and the life that is moving through us here in the present. Letting go of the pictures is surrendering that need to escape being with the experiences of life that are arising and moving through you in the moment. While you are resisting what is in the present moment, you are stuck in survival; seeking, grasping, longing to be someone and somewhere other than where you are and who you are right now. Every single moment you strive for a picture, you are rejecting who you are right here and right now and nothing will heal from this place.

We live in a world that sells us pictures every day: advertising, movies, cartoons, magazines, newspapers and, of course, social media. We see pictures everywhere advertising the 'ideal way to be': pictures of happiness, pictures of what love should look like, pictures of what freedom should look like. And they are sold to us with the assumption that in that picture is the solution to your inherent unworthiness or 'not enough-ness'.

So many advertisements aren't just selling a product; they're selling the idea of self-worth, confidence, and value. We become so attached to the images, as though it's the product we want. But it isn't really the product we want; it's the self-worth. And we want it because, in the reality in which we live, we believe that who we are right now has no worth. Attaching our longing to the fantasy 'out there' is like quenching our thirst from an empty glass: it will look like we're drinking, but it won't refresh us. It will give us what we think we want, but it will leave us longing even more, entrenching us deeper and deeper in the story, reaffirming the very emptiness we are trying to fill and fix. We become so consumed with pictures that we cannot see the life that is here right now. In our attempts to survive, we are missing life. We set ourselves up to be left empty – seeking, 'not enough' – and then we use that as evidence that the story we know ourselves to be is in fact right.

And we continue surviving.

Letting Go of Pictures

A month into my separation my attachment to being the warrior woman was dissolving quick and fast, allowing me to start seeing in a way I'd never seen before – in particular around my marriage. I realized I'd needed to be this warrior woman in order to overcompensate for the little girl who believed she was bad, unworthy and unlovable. I'd been holding on so tight to a picture of how marriage and family life should be in order to somehow save myself. If I could just create the 'happy picture', it would fix the pain and unworthiness I experienced within me from my past. I'd been so consumed with creating this picture, I'd completely failed to actually be present with my husband.

When I met him I was 32 and had been in and out of painful relationships for a decade. I wanted the picture of the 'happy life' so desperately. I had to have it, to somehow prove to myself that I was going to be okay. I needed it to mask how insecure I felt in the world and how much my heart had been broken by the past. I wanted the picture of the happy family *so much* that, when I met my husband, I was so consumed with this picture, I completely missed the possibility of the intimate, vulnerable moments of life in the present. I was so in need of this picture that I only saw the man who could potentially make the picture possible for me: I was blind to seeing him for who he actually was.

Having this moment of insight was devastating. All these years – nine years together – I'd believed I had been living presently in my life with this man, but I hadn't. My story had been living this marriage, not me. I'd been trying to live in the picture and my darling husband had been an unknown hostage in my story.

A few weeks later, my husband and I went on a family holiday – one that had been pre-planned before we separated, and we had promised the kids we'd still go. One evening, I asked him if he'd come to dinner with me. As we sat opposite each other – so much hurt and pain in both our hearts, a gaping hole between us – I looked up at him and said: 'I've realized something. I've realized that the girl I was when I met you was so consumed with wanting the picture she had in her mind – a picture I believed I needed to somehow take away my pain – that I didn't really allow us the space and time to truly see each other. I'm so sorry that, in only wanting the picture, I missed truly seeing you. You deserved to be seen and I'm so sorry that I've hurt you.'

For a moment he said nothing, as I felt the pain in his heart so deeply. Then he simply looked up with such gratitude and said thank you. A moment of peace passed between us. It was the beginning of making things whole again after all the destruction. For nine years I had not truly seen him, but now I was seeing him fully for who he was. And that was healing both for him and for me. In that moment, a part of him had been set free: the part that needed to fit the role of the man in my fantasy. He was no longer required to be the hostage in my story. By being courageous enough to surrender the picture of our marriage and let go of the life we both thought we *should* have been living, somehow we were allowing the space for something whole, something new, to come through.

It was both painful and beautiful, surrendering the hope that one day I would be Cinderella, fall madly in love with my prince, and live happily ever after. But as painful as it was, it was real and it was true and it was so authentic that in the very moment of pain there was beauty. What was to become of us was out of our hands – we just didn't know – but we knew that whatever we'd had, and whatever expectations we'd been holding on to attached to pictures, had to go now.

I'd used pictures as a way of avoiding being present with the real and true moments of my life. I'd used them since I was a little girl to escape the devastation of my childhood, desperately trying to hold on to something hopeful that would one day save me. But while I was living as though I needed to be 'saved' by something 'out there' from something I was trying to escape 'back there', I was failing to live and be with what was arising in the moment.

But life only exists here in the present, and by surrendering the fantasy and the hope of being saved, you can begin to be here now – with yourself, with who you are and where you are, right here, right now. This is your home; this is the very place you have needed to learn to be with all along. In the pain there is beauty, and in the presence there is safety, peace, warmth, contentment and love. Surrender the pictures so you can come home. The home you're longing for is the home within yourself, in the moment, in the now.

If you're truly ready to begin living your life and step out of surviving, if you're truly ready to free yourself from the well, then it is time to let go of the pictures and surrender searching and grasping and seeking. Surrender the hope of being saved, which has been diverting you away from being with who you are and where you are right now. There is no life in those pictures; there is only more suffering. Pictures will always be out there, out of reach, leaving you searching, seeking and missing the actual alive moments of your life now. The life you're searching for is already here; the one you're searching for is already here, within you now.

Let go of the pictures and be here now.

EXERCISE: YOUR PICTURES

1. What picture do you have in your mind of who you think you 'should' be, how your life is 'meant' to be, and how it 'needs' to be, in order to survive and 'fix' your past?

2. Which part of you needs to fulfil this picture? Is it your authentic self that is already enough, or the self that is living in the story? Write a few paragraphs about what is prompting your need to have this picture for life. What need is at the core? What feelings are driving it? How young are you in it? To whom are you trying to prove that the picture is fulfilled? And for what reason?

3. Reflecting on the inquiry above: is this need and drive to fulfil the picture feeding your true self or your survival? Write in your journal what arises for you at the invitation of surrender? Who or what are you really surrendering?

4. Describe in your journal 2–3 examples of times in your life when you have rejected your truth, your own experience, other people, or opportunities because they didn't fit the picture you thought you needed to live in?

5. What is it that you really want? Think back to those advertisements – is it the product that you want or the self-worth? Is this picture going to give you want you really want?

6. Now you are here, letting the picture go, write in your journal what it is you really want, beyond the pictures. Fulfilment as an artist? Deep conscious intimacy with a partner? A feeling of safety, security and peace within? You can have anything you want, as long as you're willing to let go of the picture of what you thought it should look like.

'VISIONING' MEDITATION

Close your eyes as you sit in a comfortable position. Take three deep, slow, conscious breaths in and, as you exhale, allow your body to release and let go.

Bring your awareness inwards and, slowing right down, meet yourself where you are.

As you settle into the present, bring your awareness to what you really want – to what it is that you've discovered you really want, beyond the picture. Not what you want it to look like; not what you want to get; not what you want to do; but how you want to feel and who you want to *be*, living in the present of fulfilling what you want.

Really see yourself there. Be there. Experience it with the whole of your body.

With every in-breath I invite you to experience yourself fulfilling, receiving and living fully what you want, filling up every part of your being. Maybe you want to feel secure and safe in yourself. Maybe you want to feel inspired and fulfilled reaching your full potential. Maybe you want to be a mother and have that deep connection with your child. Whatever it is, here and now, *really be there* in it as though it is happening right now. See yourself, feeling yourself, experience it in the present.

Spend 10 minutes breathing into this present state of being in your visualization.

And when the time is up, allow your breathing to regulate and open your eyes.

Write in your journal any insights or realizations or experiences that came to you during this exercise.

Telling the Truth

Within the story, all we are doing is surviving: surviving the pain, heartbreak, emptiness, loneliness – whatever the challenging human experience from the past is that we don't have the capacity to *be* with. And within the story, the character that we know ourselves to be has to fit the story, as evidence or proof of the story that is keeping us captive. But this character is not who we are; it is a character that we've created in order to survive. In our commitment to surviving, we mould, sculpt, and fit who we are into the character we've decided we need to be in order to survive. To somehow keep a sense of control over what others will think of us, how the world will see us, how life will unfold for us and everything in between. All in a subconscious attempt to ensure that we never again have to experience what we went through in our past.

As that character, we live in the world with a mask on – the mask of the character that is trying to be 'not her past' – but as long as we're living behind a mask, we're not living and the world will never meet us, connect with us, or see us for who we truly are. Because if we were to show our true selves to others and the world, we'd risk being rejected, unloved, or unwelcomed, and repeating history by having our hearts broken all over again. We abandon our truth in order to be the character in the story. We hide who we are in order to fit the mould of someone we think we should be; someone we think we need to be in order to survive our past. But our hiding is a form of self-abandonment and it is inauthentic. And it is lonely behind a mask. As long as we are hiding, we reaffirm the story that we are not enough as we are. And the more fear we have of whatever it is we are trying to survive, the more we hide our true selves and reject the truth within us right now. Entrenching us deeper into fear and disconnection and survival, this behaviour only takes us further and further away from being at home within ourselves, back on that hamster wheel that we call our life.

To live beyond the story we must surrender the mask and come out of hiding, learning to tell the truth about who we are to the world and to ourselves. To release the judgements of the fears, insecurities, doubts, imperfections, and vulnerabilities; the shadow and the light, the clumsiness and clunkiness; and the irrationality, joy, light, playfulness and wildness. All of it. To begin telling the truth is the beginning of surrendering control and the beginning of coming out of hiding.

Truth-telling Time

When I surrendered the picture of my marriage and the picture of the warrior woman, there was nothing else to lose. I found myself at a place in my life where all that was left was for me to truly be me. But who was that? As I dived deeper into this process, I realized that so

Life only exists here in the present, and by surrendering the fantasy and the hope of being saved, you can begin to be here now – with yourself, with who you are and where you are, right here, right now.

~

much of who I thought I was had been attached to those two pictures. Now that they were gone, I was faced with an entire world within me that I'd been hiding away. And hiding even from myself.

The only way forwards from this place was to start truly honouring and telling the truth of who I was and what arose within me – to myself, to my husband, to my life. By now, my husband and I were meeting each week for therapy, not to save the marriage but to heal our relationship so that we could co-parent our children with love and presence. They were both so little, so we were going to have to learn to be in each other's lives for a very long time. In our sessions, I made the promise to myself to tell the truth no matter what. Things I'd never have dared to say if I was still trying to control the outcome and, as we had nothing to lose, the freedom was there.

It was truth-telling time.

I shared that I'd been feeling trapped, and that I didn't think I was suited to conventional marriage and motherhood and all the expectations that came with these roles. I shared that I'm someone that needs a lot of my own space, and that I found the way we had been living suffocating. With every moment of truth-telling I found myself feeling more liberated – like shackles of chains falling off me so that finally I could move. I couldn't quite believe that I was actually allowed to be this person. You mean, I'm actually allowed to be fully who I am? It was like discovering an entire well of life within me that I'd been hiding, even from myself, to ensure that I'd still be loved and not abandoned by the world.

With every moment of truth-telling to myself, I was actually meeting myself for what felt like the very first time. The shedding of a mask, releasing generations and generations of pictures of who a 'worthwhile woman' needed to be versus who I truly am. With each moment of truth-telling to my husband, I was surrendering even more need to control how he felt about me. And he did the same for me. We were literally smashing apart the illusions and expectations that we had both wanted the other to be, allowing something to start flowing through that was much more subtle; much more truthful, much more intimate. A 'realness', a truth, a freedom in which we were actually allowed to be our whole entire selves, as we are.

The truth and authenticity began unfurling in every area of my life.

I was at home one day – now on my own, the kids in bed – and suddenly really seeing the walls of my bathroom. I know it may sound strange, but it was as though I'd never really seen them before and I was seeing them for the first time with new eyes. I started looking around my house and realized that I had not fully been living there. I, the whole and true me, the one that was now coming alive, had not fully been living there. So many of the choices I'd made about how the house ended up looking had been led by trying to please my husband, or in order to fit the picture of what a 'nice house' looked like.

Over the next few days, I took things down, put things up, and cleared out drawers, shelves, and cupboards. I discovered that I didn't even like at least half of my clothes, so I sent them off to charity shops. Who had I been living as all this time? Where had I been? Who was this woman birthing through me now? After a week of cleaning and clearing, I sat in my living room and took in the entire space with completely open eyes. It was like meeting my home for the very first time. A remarkable contentment rushed through me; such peace. This is what it felt like to be home; not just in my home, but at home in myself. And who I was becoming didn't feel like a bigger, better version of myself, it felt like becoming more me than I'd ever been in my whole life – remembering something I'd always known but didn't quite know how to own.

In our quest to survive, we suppress and hide so much of who we truly are in order to control how others see us. In an attempt to control the outcomes, we give up who we are, and fit ourselves to the pictures in our minds of who we have been taught and told we should be in order to survive this life. And as we move further and further away from our truth, something deep within ourselves – our soul – knows that we are out of alignment with the integrity of who we are. Something knows but we don't know how to recognize it, or trust it, or to listen to it. We just think there is something wrong with us and use that unease as evidence that who we are, as we are, is not enough. Deep down, we believe the story that if anyone were to ever truly see all that we are and all that arises within us, there simply is no way we would be loved and valued and accepted. All the fears, neediness, doubts, wildness, shyness, goofiness, clunkiness; the need for both love and freedom, the need for touch and solitude. And so we reject all our 'human-ness'. We hide ourselves away behind masks. In our quest to survive being rejected and abandoned by the world, we reject ourselves and cut off all the rich aliveness of who we truly are.

And so here we are, together at this point, and I want to ask you again: who do you wish to be when you are living beyond the story? Do you wish to be free? Do you wish to be true? Do you wish to be more *you* than you've ever been in your life before? Feel it in your body, this cannot come from your mind. All the truth of who you are is not in your mind: it is in your body, it is in your heart, it is in your soul.

If you wish to stop surviving, it is time to surrender the control, surrender the mask, and begin telling the truth of who you truly are: to yourself, to the ones you love around you, to the walls in your home, to the trees in the woods, to your life. And as you do, you'll be opening to a completely new sense of space for the real, rich abundance of the aliveness that has been within you all along, letting it flow through you and into your life.

EXERCISE: TRUTH-TELLING

1. In your journal, write a list of all the ways in which hiding yourself and your truth is serving you. For example: *I get to control how people perceive me. I get to make sure I'm not rejected.*

2. Now write a list of all the ways telling the truth about all of who you are will serve you. For example: *I get to finally be myself. I get to choose a life I love. I get to feel free.*

3. Reviewing both sets of lists, write a few paragraphs about which one is feeding your story and keeping you more stuck, and which one is feeding your healing and your authentic evolvement. Write about what you are seeing here, why and how, and describe what it brings up for you.

4. Write a Truth-telling Letter to the world and everyone you know in it. You can address it: 'Dear everyone in my world'. In the letter, I want you to describe all the things about yourself that are your truths, which you've never shared or let them see. Keep writing everything that comes to you until your letter feels thorough and complete. For example: *Dear everyone in my world, I want to share myself with you honestly and truthfully. I am in fact very*

shy, but I pretend to be noisy in case I get forgotten about and in case I won't be loved. I hate my job and dream of being a singer but I've always been too scared to admit that to myself or anyone....

5. When you have finished writing the letter, read it aloud to yourself. And if you're feeling very brave, read it to someone you love and trust. Write in your journal anything that comes up for you from this exercise.

6. Write 3–5 actions you are willing to take to start honouring what is really truthful to you, and that has been out of alignment with truth in your life.

7. Write another vision – 24 hours in a day of being you telling the absolute truth and living aligned with your truth.

Being Comfortable with Uncomfortable

There aren't that many times when I say that something is absolutely guaranteed. But this is one of those times. If you want the freedom that comes with being your authentic self and living beyond the story, I'm afraid you are going to have to learn how to become more comfortable with the uncomfortable. The very nature of the story is about resistance; about doing, and having, and getting somewhere other than where we are right now. Strategies to get away from or fix the human experience that is arising in the present and thus removing us from the present. And what we call our life is what is in between, trying to get somewhere in order to get away from somewhere. So to truly surrender this way of being and existing, we need to learn to be with the human experiences that arise in the here and now. Of course, what will arise first is often all that we have been resisting over the years until now. What we resist persists, so to heal is to be with all that we have resisted, which I'm afraid can be extremely uncomfortable.

Honestly, I can't think of a single person I've worked with to whom I haven't had to say this same thing I'm saying to you now: your ability to live truly connected to the present, with a sense of peace and freedom aligned with what is whole and authentic for you, lies in your ability to be comfortable with the uncomfortable. This is not about feeling better – it is not about fixing – this is about healing and about becoming free.

Exposed

Five months after returning from my first trip to Peru, as part of my commitment to living beyond my story, I attended my first big transformational programme at The Concord Institute in London. Three days into a three-month process, I stood up to share myself with the group. I don't remember exactly what words I used, but I remember saying something about my early childhood I'd never shared with anyone before, let alone spoken aloud to a group of 30 strangers and four facilitators.

As I was speaking, I started having this deeply uncomfortable experience of being completely exposed. It was as if someone had taken off the top layer of my skin and my heart was laid bare for all to see and scrutinize. It was so uncomfortable I started fidgeting and twitching and shuffling my feet back and forth, until eventually I almost bolted out of the room. The facilitator saw instantly something was going on for me and asked me to describe what was moving through me. I told her how raw and exposed I felt and how much I wanted to run. Her response has stayed with me to this day: 'Nicky, feeling exposed is a sign that you are sharing the truth. It is a sign that you are not hiding, and allowing your truth to be witnessed. Isn't that what you actually want?'

She was right. It is what I'd always wanted: to be seen and accepted and at home with who I truly am. But bloody hell, I hadn't realized it would be so uncomfortable doing it. I'd realized that all the survival strategies – the whole warrior-woman character – had been about protecting myself from that raw exposure which I'd equated with being attacked, criticized and judged. But in escaping that danger I was moving further and further away from what I truly wanted. So, there and then, I had a choice: do what I'd always done – run away, distract, hide so I didn't have to feel the uncomfortableness – or surrender and be with it, no matter what.

Guess what I chose? The experience was unbearably uncomfortable but it didn't actually kill me. And the more I let it be without running, the more present I found myself becoming.

I realized that this must be how it felt to be seen, to be vulnerable, and to be present in the here and now. I felt alive and present and soft and actually there, while simultaneously being with the 'uncomfortableness' of the suppressed fear and shame from the past. Painful and beautiful; uncomfortable and free.

Ten years on, during truth-telling time with my husband, things were starting to get excruciatingly uncomfortable. Each time I told the truth, I was allowing my true self to be seen and exposing myself. It felt scary, vulnerable, risky, dangerous but equally it felt free. Each time I exposed myself, I felt a rush of past fears and shame and unworthiness move through me. The old pain of being abandoned, humiliated, shamed, and rejected moved through me like waves rushing in and out of the shore. Deeply, deeply uncomfortable. But I continued committing, being with it no matter what.

Then something profound started to shift.

After five months without a moment's doubt that we were finished as a couple and heading straight for divorce, and despite doubting that we'd ever even be able to be friends, somehow we had a huge breakthrough. A softness started showing up between us. A completely fresh, new experience of care and kindness; a stillness and spaciousness and a feeling of ease that we had never had before. And in that stillness and spaciousness, we found ourselves able to listen to each other in a way we hadn't been able to before. I could see him much more clearly and, if he got reactive, instead of just seeing the anger and reaction and immediately feeling threatened and shutting myself down, I could see past it and see his vulnerability, his fear, his pain. This led me to speak to him differently and show up for him in a completely new way. Every moment I was able to be with the uncomfortableness that moved through me, more of the walls of protection around me dissolved and a new unplanned, unseen possibility birthed through. As a result, we began building a friendship and it felt really good.

In all our resisting and fixing and avoiding of what is uncomfortable, we miss the life that is arising in the present. It is in the present, while being with the life moving through us, that we surrender enough of the fight to create a spaciousness that can allow a new possibility – new life, a new story – to flow through. Being comfortable with the uncomfortable is surrendering survival in order for life to unfurl; shifting from doing our life to being a space for life to flow through.

The more life that can flow through, the more new possibilities open for us.

EXERCISE: BEING UNCOMFORTABLE

1. Think about all the strategies you use to avoid feeling uncomfortable. List in your journal as many ways that you can think of right now.

2. What is truly the most uncomfortable experience for you? Is it intimacy? Being seen? Being given attention? Being shamed? Write a few paragraphs about what for you are the most uncomfortable experiences you can imagine.

3. Now explore whether these directly correlate to what you actually really want. For example: *I want deep, connected relationships. But intimacy, being seen, being out of control, are all deeply uncomfortable for me.* Write in more depth about the connections between what is uncomfortable versus what you really want.

4. Can you see that what you want is on the other side of you learning to be able to be uncomfortable without reacting or escaping? Are you ready and willing to allow yourself to be uncomfortable, to let it move through you in commitment to fulfilling what you want?

BODYWORK: BEING WITH

This exercise is particularly powerful if you can do it with someone else, but if you can't do that, you can do it with yourself looking in a mirror. The intention is to hold eye contact for the full 10 minutes as you allow whatever experiences arise and fall within you.

I invite you to set a timer for 10 minutes so you don't need to keep checking the time.

Sit cross-legged on the floor or on a flat surface. If you're doing this with someone else, face each other directly, with eyes at the same level. Sit close enough to each other so that your knees are just touching – not so close that you feel squashed, but not so far away that it feels distant. If you are doing this on your own, sit directly facing a mirror so that you can look into your own eyes.

Once in position, take a deep breath and begin to hold eye contact. Don't stare each other down but do hold eye contact for the duration of the exercise.

If anything starts to move through you, allow it to come and allow it to go.

If you find yourself desperate to lower your eyes as much as possible, acknowledge how uncomfortable it makes you feel but continue holding eye contact. Do not bail on your partner or on yourself. Stay here for the full 10 minutes.

When the time is up, release your eyes and share with each other how it was.

Describe in your journal any insights, seeings or 'aha!' moments you learned from this.

Listening Beyond Ears

My client Natasha called me one morning in a panic, gripped within the walls of her story. Fear and panic filled her every pore; her face pained with worry and doubt, her mind filled with the narrative from her past. She was in the midst of birthing a new work project and had a very tight deadline to meet. From where she was standing in that moment, deep in the trenches of her own story, she was so stuck that she couldn't see a way forwards. The only possibility she could see before her was one of disaster – one in which she'd finally lose control, her whole dream would collapse around her, and her world would collapse with it.

When Natasha was a little girl, her mother had become very unwell, and witnessing her health deteriorate was an experience that Natasha relives in body and mind over and over again. Natasha's story is that she'll lose everything she loves, so every time she tries to create something she loves or to nurture a dream, this story reactivates and she's back in the well. When Natasha is in the story she cannot imagine any possibility other than the one she always expects – the one where everything falls apart.

On that call, I helped her surrender the resistance and start being with the experience moving through her. Panic, terror, heartbreak, powerlessness. She closed her eyes, took a deep breath, and let go of trying to resist and run away from the feelings, Instead, she allowed herself to simply be with the uncomfortableness of it all. The more she surrendered to what was rising, the more still she became, and the more she returned to being in the present. Slowly the panic and fear and terror started to dissolve and she became much quieter. Her breath dropped deeper and her mind quietened.

I asked her what she was experiencing now.

'Sadness and fear,' she said.

I asked her how young she was in that moment.

'Six years old,' she replied

And so I asked her to simply be with that six-year-old child.

Not trying to fix the child; change her, judge her, make her better. Just to be with her.

After a little time I could sense her whole being become quiet and she told me: 'I feel still. The sadness and fear is still there but the six-year-old has calmed down and so have I.'

As she opened her eyes, she seemed completely different to how she'd been when she first came on the call. Grounded, present, anchored, with much more energy and power moving through her. Why? Because she was fully in the present and life only exists here in the present.

We then turned our focus to her work project, and I asked her to listen for any possibilities that opened up to her from where she was now. By the next day, she'd heard multiple actions she wanted to take, multiple pieces of writing she wanted to create, and she'd even felt a call to contact someone who could work with her to help promote the project to many more people. How and where did these ideas and openings come from? They had always been there, but she hadn't been able to see them or hear them from the space she was in. Looking and listening but stuck in the story, all she could hear was the story, and we can only hear life from the space beyond the story. Also, the possibility that Natasha could be at ease – in the flow, abundantly and effortlessly creating, anchored and connected to the present – so starkly conflicted with the story with which she'd been identifying, such a possibility simply wasn't available to her while she was stuck in the well.

To allow the possibility of a new unfolding, we need to be listening from a space beyond the story. When we are stuck in the story, all we can hear is a narrative that aligns with the story. Natasha's experience is typical of thousands I could share with you, Including my own: the experience of a completely unknown, unseen possibility that opens up when we begin to listen from a place beyond the story and beyond the noise.

Listening is only listening if you are listening from a space in which there is an unknown outcome. Listening is no longer listening when you already know what is always going to happen. Listening is no longer listening if there is a predetermined, pre-planned, projected answer already. Most of the time we are not listening. We may be hearing noise, but that's not the same as listening. Within the story there is no listening, because all we hear is the narrative that's always already there, pre-programmed from memories in the past. It's like being in a conversation with someone who acts like they're listening, but who's really just waiting to say what they've already decided they're going to say, regardless of any input from you.

This is what we're doing with our life: acting like we're listening, but really having already decided how it's going to unfold, led by the narrative of the story in our mind. Letting go of pictures opens us up into the unknown; in the unknown uncomfortableness arises. Surrendering resistance and escape to be with uncomfortableness allows life to move through us, dissolving the attachment that the reaction and story has for us. And allowing us to drop deeper into being in the present moment.

Being with the past arising in the present is only possible beyond the mind, and beyond the mind there is no language, no story, no noise, no narrative, no always already knowing. Beyond the mind there is only stillness and space, and this is where we can truly begin listening. Listening to what? Well actually, it's not so much *what* you're listening to, because beyond the mind is silence: it's more *where* you are listening from. Listening from spaciousness, from stillness, where there are no pictures, no answers, you are not the character and there is no story.

This space, between where you are and the noise of the mind, is where all new creative possibility can unfold. Remember when I said in the Introduction that I now find myself in a beautiful dance with life – a dance in which neither of us knows what the next steps will be, we just need to listen to the music? Here, in this space, beyond the story, is where I want you to listen from – in order to hear the music, in order to know what the next steps need to be, in order to listen to life.

Being, Not Doing

Like being rather than doing, listening is not passive. It is alive and active. In fact, true listening requires all your presence and awareness, as there's not *nothing* happening during listening, there's *everything* happening – but you need to be awake to hear it and see it. There are many names used for this space of listening: deeper wisdom, intuition, deeper knowing, inner truth, life, Source, spirit, the universe. I believe it to be all of these things. An active mutual exchange of presence and co-creation between your deep inner wisdom and life. No predetermined outcome; only an alive, flowing space of possibility. You may wonder how this can be available to you, but have you ever noticed that you get your best ideas in the shower? Or while walking alone in nature? Or maybe while you're washing up or knitting or drawing. These are moments when you've managed to separate yourself enough from attachment to the mind; these are moments when openings can occur.

Learn to listen from here and you open up the possibility of creating anything you dream. Beyond the story, beyond the mind, beyond who you thought you were. Aligned with life.

EXERCISE: LISTENING

How much have you needed to be the one that is 'knowing'? How much has this got in the way of you actually listening?

1. List in your journal 3–5 examples of occasions in your life when your 'knowing' has got in the way of you being able to listen.

2. What were the consequences that arose as a result? Write a few paragraphs on the full unfolding that resulted from this behaviour.

3. What do you feel is at the root and core of your need to *know*? Write down what you think is getting in the way of you really listening.

4. When you connect to what you really want, where can you see your guidance coming from? Does it come from a picture? If not, where?

5. Begin to really listen in your life. When someone is speaking with you, notice whether you've already decided you know what they're saying and therefore 'checked out' mentally. Bring your awareness to actively listening to every word someone's saying.

Listen to what's not being spoken through words but being spoken in other ways. Listen to the space behind the words. This will require you to slow right down.

6. Use your journal to capture all that comes up for you from this exercise.

BODYWORK: WALKING

At least three times in the next week, go for a good walk, at least 20–30 minutes long. Walk in nature if possible, but if you can't get to a park or nature then just walk.

But with no distractions – no music, no phones, no one else but you. Walk in complete silence and bring your awareness to the present. Be aware of every single step you take as your foot comes off the ground and returns back to the ground.

Walk slowly, consciously. Make sure you're taking nice, deep, slow breaths. As much as possible, relax and let your belly completely hang out.

Walk this practice regularly. In particular, walk it at times when your mind has become noisy and you need to hear an answer from a more authentic space of wisdom.

After your walks, return to your journal and write down any insights or learnings you've gained.

PHASE 3

A Birthing

The creation of life appears the

moment you choose life.

～

CHAPTER 6
Living to Thrive

'Surrender your fear. Something will come that is greater than what the fear is trying to protect.'

MOOJI

Six months after the separation, my six-year-old daughter asked if we could have a chat. I knew instantly from her tone something was bothering her so I invited her to speak freely about what was in her heart. These were her words: 'Mummy, I've been thinking a lot lately and I'm worried about falling in love. I've decided I don't want it to happen.'

When I asked her why, she replied: 'Well, because what if I fall in love and we break up like you and Daddy have and I have to feel as much pain as you are feeling? What if we fight like you and Daddy have? Falling in love seems scary because it seems to hurt so much. I'd rather not do it at all.'

My heart blew open for my daughter. So young, but wise beyond her years. And speaking so much truth that there wasn't anything I could say to discount what she was seeing. So I replied: 'Darling one, what you are seeing is very true. To love deeply means to risk that your heart may also experience loss and pain and disappointment. But even though your father and I have ended up where we are, I still wouldn't go back and change any of it, because I gave my whole heart and I'm still giving my whole heart and that's what it means to be alive. If you live your life trying to make sure you don't get hurt or experience disappointment, you will not be living. You will miss all the things that make being alive so wonderful. To experience deep love, joy, play, freedom, excitement, adventure, creativity – you cannot have these moments without taking a risk. Disappointment is part of life, my darling, and each time it comes you will grow a little stronger and a little wiser than before, so don't hold back. Live this life like you're living to win, instead of living to not lose.'

Her sweet little face lit up as I witnessed the possibility of play, love and freedom return to her.

This struggle is what so many of us find ourselves trapped in. The terror of experiencing hurt, disappointment, rejection, and pain causes us to hold ourselves back so much that we don't even try. In our attempt to protect ourselves, we are suffocating our lives from aliveness, allowing the fears of our minds and memories of the past to inhibit our freedom to truly live with a full, open heart. This is not living. This is surviving. And surviving has nothing to do with living. Surviving is merely about not dying, and a fundamental part of the process of surrendering our attachment to the survival story involves shifting the relationship we have with fear.

At the core of our childhood wounds and trauma is some form of broken heart – some point in our past when we experienced a crushing disappointment that really, really hurt. In fact, as children we'd have experienced it as our entire world crumbling around us. Perhaps the moment we realize our mother and father aren't perfect and they've let us down, or losing a dearly loved pet that was our best friend. Moments of being laughed at in school or, like my daughter, a moment of realizing that love comes hand in hand with pain. All moments when we realize that life isn't a perfect, happy, safe bubble.

These moments in childhood are exceptionally painful and they're all moments of trauma. Not the trauma we see in movies, of car crashes and violence, but the trauma of realizing that the world is not as we thought it was and who we are in it may not be safe. Trauma is not what happens to us; it's what happens inside us and what meaning we then give to what's happening inside us. This is what is traumatic. In these moments, who we are in the world and how we experience life is under threat, and everything in our experience of reality and who we think we are in the world can change in a second.

The nature of childhood innocence is to live in a world that we believe is pure and perfect and whole and trustworthy, and we're wholly reliant on this world to keep us alive. And at the core of human nature is a deep desire to love and to be loved. Our parents are our first loves; they are our whole world.

These moments of shock, trauma and splitting are our first experiences of the painful knowledge that what comes hand in hand with love is also the threat of loss and heartbreak. And so we split – in this moment of threat we subconsciously begin finding ways to survive. Our minds take over and create a whole story, in which we are the main character, with the sole purpose of ensuring we never experience that pain again.

We dedicate our lives to living 'not pain'. Instead of living to win, we are living to 'not lose'.

My daughter was on a fast track to living a life in which she would never have fully opened her heart again, because in her story love had become a dangerous thing. Thankfully, I was able to sit with her to dismantle that story. But she will probably create another one about something else and I won't catch them all, because it is human nature to have stories and minds. The exciting part of being human is to begin dismantling these stories and waking up to who we truly are. Remember: this is our destiny and it's in our essential nature to grow and mature.

When I'm panicking about my children having stories, my teacher David will say: 'Well, they have to have something to work on in this life.' When we're in the story, we are not using our lives to win; we are using them to 'not lose', always ready to block any and every possibility of having a chance to live fully.

Befriending Disappointment

Disappointment is part of being alive. We cannot love or care about anything or allow ourselves to want anything without risking the possibility of being disappointed. So we must choose. A life based on doing whatever we can to avoid disappointment, and therefore also based on blocking love, connection, freedom and dreams? Or transforming our relationship with fear so that we can learn to live and accept being with disappointment as a necessary part of truly living? Life can be a torture chamber or the greatest education of all. With every moment of pain, challenge, rejection, or disappointment comes an opportunity to learn more about ourselves and about life. An opportunity to evolve and mature. Without risking disappointment and living to win, our lives have so much less meaning – no challenge, just getting by. Sadly, this is the trade-off so many people are making today.

What would become of your life if disappointment was an important part of learning and growth? What if each disappointment was a reminder of how much you've cared, how much you've loved, how much you've chosen living over surviving? Within the story, disappointment is used as evidence that the story is right, entrenching us even deeper in survival. Within the story, we are always already expecting some form of disappointment, because this will corroborate our assumptions about the world. It will validate for us that who we've always known ourselves to be and how we see the world is 'right', so that we can continue to justify our decision to stay small, stay hidden, protect ourselves and survive. And not take the risk of truly living.

But at what cost? Back to that conversation with my six-year-old. Her options were: I will not give my heart ever to anyone, and therefore I will not truly love, to make sure I never experience heartbreak or pain; or: I will learn to be with what it means to be alive, able to be comfortable with uncomfortableness in service of truly living.

You are the same as my daughter. We all are. If we slow down enough to inquire why we're so afraid of disappointment, what would we see? We'd see fear of pain, fear of heartbreak, fear of not being able to have the picture we had so wanted to save us, fear of not being able to control. Fear. Fear is simply another human experience that we can learn to be with. Fear is not the problem; it is our resistance to being with fear and what we make it mean that is the problem. That's what shuts down our hearts and blocks our soul's desire to thrive, cutting off everything that signifies being human and being alive. If we're committed to being with fear and pain, and with all the experiences of life that move through, and if we're committed to letting go of pictures and telling the truth of who we are, then does experiencing fear seem so bad?

No Guarantees

We want so much to have a guarantee that if we take action, if we leap, if we go for what we want, if we follow our hearts and dreams, it's all going to be okay. No such guarantee can ever be given, however, so the risk is very real. This leaves us with two essential questions to weigh up for ourselves: *Am I willing to not risk and to stay where I am, being in survival?*; or: *Am I willing to take the risk, leap into the unknown in service of my heart's desires, without any guarantee but opening the possibility of living to win?*

Living to win is a new relationship with our lives; one in which the process of living itself is far more important than how it ends up looking in the end. It is an active commitment of honouring truth, listening to our hearts, and taking risks in order to follow life's dream for us. Living to win is responding to the deeper listening within and trusting that actions taken from this place are aligned with what is authentic and true to who we are. And that is all that really matters in life. Living to win is about love; about acting from love, not fear. Love for ourselves and love for our lives. Living to not lose is fear and only fear. We cannot control the outcomes but we can control how we live and we can control how we wish to be.

And there will come a point at which you decide that survival just can't be an option any more. Once you've popped your head over the top of the well and seen the beauty and gift of what is possible for yourself and your life. When that time comes, and you're ready to surrender and take the risk in service of what is unknown but authentic and true, then your life and how you use it takes on a whole new depth of meaning.

When this time comes (which I'm hoping is right now as you read this book), it will feel as though you've jumped out of a building. Fear will move through you and it will be uncomfortable. But then it will pass and you'll begin to see that living this way is actually living, and surviving will no longer be an option any more. Do you think, after the frog saw the expansive, limitless world out there, he decided to ignore it and continue living in the well until he died? No! He bloody learned how to get the hell out of there and had a bloody great life!

And let me tell you a little secret.

When you leap, when the time comes, you may just discover that, somehow and somewhere along the way, you've learned how to fly.

EXERCISE: BEFRIENDING DISAPPOINTMENT

1. What relationship do you have with disappointment or rejection? Write a few paragraphs about this relationship in your journal.

2. Now have a look at what you have written and see if this perception is coming from a place of the character/story? How and why? Note your answers in your journal.

3. If you were living beyond the story, what could your relationship to disappointment shift to? Describe in a few paragraphs how this could impact your life?

4. If you were willing to be with disappointment and trust that it comes and passes, what actions and steps would you take in your life that you are not taking now? What dreams or visions would you leap for? Describe them in as much detail as you wish.

'GOLDEN VIBRATION AND EXPANSION' MEDITATION

Close your eyes and take three deep breaths in. Slow down and meet yourself where you are.

As you start to breathe in, visualize drawing in golden vibrational light from the Earth all the way up through your groin, your lower belly, and your abdomen, filling your whole abdomen. Let it go all the way up to your heart, filling your heart with this immense golden vibrational light. As you exhale, just let go.

Breathing in again, draw up this golden vibrational light to feed and nourish the insides of your entire being, bringing it up to your heart and expanding your heart with this golden vibration. Let go again as you exhale.

With every in-breath, draw up even more of this golden vibrational light, expanding you from the inside out, expanding the heart so bright.

Continue this cycle for a good 5–10 minutes until you are a big golden vibration of light – light bursting from every pore of you; bursting from your heart so that it's burning bright like the sun. You are now an absolute whole expression of golden frequency of light.

With your next in-breath, let the vibrational light shining from you reach everyone you love.

With your next in-breath, let the vibrational light shine and reach everyone you don't love.

With your next in-breath, let the vibrational light shine and reach your whole country.

With your next in-breath, let the vibrational light shine and reach the whole planet.

With your next in-breath, let the vibrational light shine and reach Infinity. And breathe in this magnificent space that you are and that you offer. You are here to love. You are here to connect.

Experience yourself living to win. Living to shine so bright.

And now start allowing your breathing to regulate, and your awareness to return to the present. Don't let your vibration get smaller as you open your eyes.

Write in your journals any insights that came to you from this.

Unconditional Holding

When my husband and I began building a friendship again, I noticed something substantially different occurring – not necessarily for him, but for me. All the usual moments that used to trigger me before we separated just didn't seem to bother me so much now. On one particular day I invited him to spend the evening, which in itself felt deeply vulnerable and exposing, as I was allowing myself to want to be close to him again and letting him see that I wanted to be close to him again. He lovingly declined and said he wasn't ready. I immediately felt a rush of shame and sadness move through me – the young abandoned child within popped her sweet little head up to the surface. But instead of being pulled into the story, I held space for the little child with love and presence. I simply stood there, being with all that moved through me with love and compassion, as I told him that I understood completely. We hugged and he left. Afterwards, I was quite surprised at how things were able to unfold so differently between us – no drama, no suffering, no fighting. A completely new possibility presented itself, not just between us but for myself. I was showing up in a new, more empowered way and it was rippling its powerful effects through my life. I was coming to life in a completely new and beautiful way.

And then, one month later, a really *big* shift occurred.

I went to stay with my mother over Christmas. She has pretty bad OCD, so in the past having me to stay with both children would have been a recipe for major trigger-time. But we're not in the past, we are here now, so that's good. For the first few days, I was pretty much on guard, just waiting for things to get uncomfortable and tense. For some reason, however, the usual tension – the build-up that would eventually lead to the one big holiday argument – well, it just didn't come. I was really quite surprised.

It was like living in an alternate reality, and I was curious as to why and how I was experiencing things so differently. There were multiple times when my mother got overtired and extremely cranky and then snapped at me or the kids, which in the past would have always triggered me to feel unsafe and then angry. But this time I didn't feel unsafe at all. In fact, for the first time I could see beyond her anger and see how tired she was, how vulnerable she was, and how her behaviour had nothing to do with me.

At one point, she started getting quite tough on my daughter about discipline, which in the past would have triggered me like crazy, as it reminded me of how my own childhood had felt. But this time, I saw how stressed it made her to be around mess, and how vulnerable she was behind her cranky words. Instead of fighting her, I found myself asking her to be softer with my daughter and acknowledging how challenging it must be for her to have the chaos around. She was so moved by me supporting her and seeing her beyond judgement, beyond reaction, that her walls dissolved in front of me and her heart burst open.

It carried on like this for the entire trip. I didn't get triggered once, we never argued, and for the first time in my 40 years on this Earth I experienced a profoundly loving, nurturing, unconditional bond with my mamma. To this day our relationship has never gone back to the way it used to be. At the age of 40, I now have a mamma who I love with all my heart and by whom I feel deeply loved in return.

Now let me ask you: how was this possible? Two human beings who have spent 40 years in a challenging, painful dynamic together. How did we start relating to each other so differently? She hasn't changed much, she still struggles with all the problems she's always had within herself, but because I'm standing in a new place – a place beyond the wounded, unlovable, unworthy story – it has completely shifted how she appears to me and how I occur to her.

Returning home from that trip, I was profoundly impacted by how much had shifted and was really interested in what it was that had enabled this new possibility to appear for me. Then I realized it was this: the whole time I was there, in the most sensitive space possible for triggering me right back into my story, I had instead held a completely available and unconditional space for myself. I'd allowed the mind-noise to move through with non-attachment, being with the feelings moving through, and had committed fully to being with whatever uncomfortableness arose within me. My full commitment to not resisting or running away from the experiences, along with my awareness of the story I'd been in and my awareness of the survival strategy I used to exist in, both gifted me enough spaciousness to stand in a place beyond it all and to hold an unwavering present space for myself.

A space I'd spent my whole life searching for – through boyfriends, best friends, jobs, money, looks, anything and everything. A space I'd been hungry for since I was a four-year-old little girl.

All the hungry child within me had ever wanted was to be held in a safe, loving, unconditional, available holding in which she was loved, seen, acknowledged and safe. In the past 40 years I'd never found this when I'd searched for it outside myself – nothing that lasted for more than a few brief moments of time. This time, because it was *me* holding the space for me, in the very moments I'd normally have resisted – escaped, reacted, dived deep back into the well – I didn't. In fact, I did the opposite. In those exact moments, the old story was dissolving while a new story was writing itself: one in which I trust myself, I am safe, I am worthwhile, and I am enough.

Becoming an unconditionally available holding space for ourselves offers us the safe space we all seek – and not just in a surface-level way. To commit to holding that space for ourselves – no matter what is rising, no matter how uncomfortable, no matter how much into the unknown we are diving – is an extraordinary act of love. And in the exact moment of doing so we are not in the mind, we are in the present, and that is where we access our true, authentic power.

The whole purpose of the story is to survive. It's a strategy to keep us safe against whatever it is in our past we are running from. But it's a survival strategy that blocks out life and love and freedom. This is what becomes available for you when you are standing and living beyond the story. You are the one you've been searching for the whole time. The safety – the home you've been searching for – is not and never has been out there. It is you and it needs to be you. Your past is not your fault, but what *is* your responsibility is what you carry from it that is blocking you from being fully alive and authentic and present in your life, now and in your future. When you have this kind of unconditional relationship with yourself in which you can stay rock-solid – present, available, loving, holding for all that you feel, all that you think, all that arises within you, with awareness and seeing that it is not who you are – then there will no longer be any need to survive. It's only here in the present where life and love is available to you. It's in the present that you'll come to life again.

Sadly, we cannot change the past. There were probably many times when you were let down, hurt or abandoned by people you loved, relied on or trusted. That was real and true and must be honoured fully for what it is. The story you have lived is unique to you, and you must learn not just to own every single moment of it but to live with it fully.

Now, however, you have the opportunity to live with that story with presence rather than living disconnected and disassociated from it.

And each time you do, you are healing both the past and the present in the exact same moment. Each time you are able to be with the past that rises in the present, you are dissolving the survival and opening to the life that you already are. Each time you choose to stay present with it and not push it away – not run or resist or escape or survive or pretend to be anyone else or anywhere else other than where you are – you are showing up as someone you can rely on, trust and feel safe with.

Right here, right now, you need someone to hold an unconditional space for you. Someone who won't repeat the patterns of your past; who won't abandon you, hurt you, or let you down. Someone on whom you can rely and build trust. Part of your maturation is to grow out of the child and into your full, whole, mature self. This is your opportunity to grow into the person you were born to be: beyond trauma, beyond survival, beyond the story – aligned, authentic, whole, present, alive. From this place, life will begin to appear differently for you. Nothing much will have changed, yet everything will be different, because where you'll be standing and seeing from will be different. When you make this unconditional stand for yourself, you'll approach your life – as I did – in such a way that you won't recognize who you are and yet you are more you than you've ever been.

It's like coming home. Growing out of who you thought you were (the character) and into who you were born to be all along.

EXERCISE: A SPACE FOR YOURSELF

1. What relationship do you have with the concept of holding a space for yourself? Have you in the past abandoned and rejected yourself in search of someone else to rescue you? Have you been

so hooked on surviving, you haven't been there for yourself? In continuous journalling, describe as many examples as you can of how living in your story has led you to not be there for yourself.

2. How has this impacted on the relationships in your life? How has this impacted on your dreams? How has this impacted on your peace, happiness and freedom?

3. Are you ready now to surrender this behaviour and be in an unconditional space for yourself? Just as you are right now?

4. If you still feel hesitation and resistance, who do you need to forgive or what do you need to let go of in order to allow yourself to be unconditional with yourself? Remember the contract you signed at the beginning of this book.

'INNER CHILD' MEDITATION

Sit cross-legged with your back supported or lie down. Take three deep, slow breaths into your body and with each exhale simply let go.

Bring your awareness to the present moment and meet yourself where you are right now.

With your in-breath I invite you now to breathe in with such softness, such tenderness, that the breath itself is nourishing and loving you from the inside out. Exhale and simply release.

Again, breathe in the softest, most tender, loving, nourishing breath. Exhale and release.

Continue this breathing cycle for five minutes and consciously invite your whole being to relax and soften.

Now bring your hands to your heart and say these words: 'I see you. I hold you. I love you. I'm here.' Allow yourself to breathe and receive the love.

Bring your hands to another part of your body and repeat the same words, giving space to receive the love.

Continue this practice until you have held space for all of your being, allowing yourself always to receive fully.

When you have completed the practice, say thank you to yourself and bring your awareness back to the present. Gently open your eyes.

Write in your journal any learnings or insights that arose in this meditation.

EXERCISE: POSTING A PROMISE

1. Write a letter to your inner child. Tell your inner child everything they have ever needed to hear. Acknowledge everything they have gone through and experienced and struggled with. Encourage and reassure them in a way they really and truly need.

2. At the end of the letter, make a promise (*and you must mean it*) that you are going to be there for them unconditionally from this point forwards.

3. Put the letter in an envelope, addressed to yourself. Stick a stamp on it and post it to yourself. It will be wonderful when you receive it.

CHAPTER 7

A New Possibility

*'Everything in your life is there as a vehicle
for your transformation. Use it!'*

RAM DASS

I want to return to the distinction between healing and fixing. Fixing implies that there's an answer to be found that will solve the problem once and for all. Once fixed, there is nothing more that needs to be done or looked at. The job is done. You are fixed. But then what? Fixing is so limiting: once 'fixed', there is nowhere else to go – except, of course, back to where you were before the problem. Basically, to stay the same.

Can you sense how finite that is – how fixing offers no more aliveness, no more growth, no more evolving, no more life? Fixing is static, like pictures, and fixing will only keep you where you are or take you back to where you were.

But can it create a new possibility?

Healing is alive; an ever-flowing, moving, evolving flow of life. Healing starts from where you were and creates a process of metamorphosis in which the old grows into something new that flows even more abundantly than before. Healing is limitless. Healing is a way to live this life that allows for the constant creation of new possibility to grow from the old. The old becomes the new and the new can only exist by having grown from the old.

The new appears at the exact moment the old dissolves. They are not separate from each other; they exist because of each other, and are only possible simultaneously but not distinct from each other.

And why am I telling you this?

Because there'll come a time when you're living beyond the story and you'll begin experiencing your full whole and authentic self. You'll be out of survival, beyond the noise of the mind, holding space for all that arises within you, with no attachment to the story. An aliveness will move through you and from you that allows the people and the world around you to appear in a new way. Beyond the 'same old same old' of the hamster-wheel story you've always known. A new possibility. Your head will be above the top of the well and a whole new world will become available to you. It'll feel amazing, and you'll want to hold on to it for dear life because it feels so good, but at some point the noise of your mind will become loud again and the story will show itself again. This does not mean you've failed and that you should pack the whole thing in.

That mindset belongs in the world of fixing, because in the fixing world your story will be gone now and the character will never return and, like Cinderella and the prince, you can live happily ever after. But you're not here to be fixed. You're here to heal and live a fully aligned and extraordinary life with limitless possibility.

We cannot be human without having an identity, and that identity is the character called 'me'. The very nature of being human is to have a 'me' that exists in the story, and so the story will not just be plucked out of you and removed forever (which is often the hope!). Our freedom does not lie in the story being plucked out and removed. Our freedom lies in our ability to live with the story while knowing we are not the story. Our freedom lies in our ability to live beyond the story while having a story.

So often, people think that freedom lies in the ability to be beyond human somehow; that if we can just live as energy or meditate our way to the sky, we'll finally be free. But the only way that really works is if we're willing to no longer exist in the world of human beings and go live on a mountain top. It's a beautiful existence for some, but most of us still need to learn how to be here: on Earth, in life, in relationships as human beings. To achieve this with freedom and power and presence and alignment is to live beyond the story while having a story. It's releasing your attachment to the story while simultaneously standing in a space with the story. The more we recognize the attachment we have to survival – to the story – the less power it has over who we are and how we live, until soon it becomes like a quiet radio playing in the next room. You can hear it and you're aware of it, but it no longer has any power or hold over you.

One does not need to replace the other. You can live beyond the story while being with the story. Simultaneously. The story and character are still part of who you are, but they are not all of who you are. Just as you can be with the life experiences that arise within you in the present, you can also learn to be with the story and the character as it appears, while simultaneously coming from this space beyond the story.

There is a difference between being *in* your story and being *with* your story. This phenomenon makes no sense to the rational mind, because to say that something is and is not at the same time does not make sense to the mind. The mind functions only on a conceptual level, but this cannot be possible on a conceptual level; it can only be experienced and lived. Zen masters call this phenomenon 'double exposure': to see you as the character in the story and you as not the character in the story, both simultaneously. One can only exist because of the other, and vice versa – like the process of healing.

Co-creating a New Reality

Let me help you understand this more deeply by telling you a story. Over the course of a few months, my husband and I had begun creating a friendship. Learning how to be with each other with no expectations other than to be with each other as our full, whole, individual selves. It was such a sweet and beautiful experience. There was something so peaceful – so freeing – in having taken away all expectation of having to be anything for the other. We'd taken away all the ties and expectations that came with sex and love and marriage. All there was now was to show up as ourselves – him being him, me being me – learning to be with each other in this new way. Some nights we'd put the kids to bed, then cook together and sit and eat a meal together. Some days we spoke on the phone; other days we didn't. Simple everyday things that seemed to be remarkable and beautiful.

And there was really no expectation for it. Maybe this was it – we'd be friends in our life – or maybe it would grow. The more we stayed in the here and now, the more free it became. It felt sweet, peaceful, gentle and alive, all at the same time. And somehow, now I look back on it, in those exact moments when we were giving each other the full allowance to be our whole selves, with complete freedom and no expectation, while being with each other in this new way, a completely new, unknown relationship began to appear. Not one after the other; not one replacing the other. It was simultaneous. One could not have been possible without the existence of the other. Because we were giving full allowance of who we are and being with it, a new possibility appeared in the present moment of being with each other. We were not striving to make something or be something or reach somewhere. We were simply being with each other and, in that presence, something new was being born. In the present moments of seeing him, hearing him, being with him, and him being the same with me, I found a love growing within my heart for him in a way I'd never experienced before. And he felt the same for me.

If we'd tried to force it, fix it, push it or drive it in any way, I don't think this new possibility would have shown itself. It was born only from our complete surrender of all control and in service to the complete freedom of being with all that was present, with non-attachment and no expectation. In this way we found love between us again. And in the exact moment of this new love becoming available, we were still being with the other as our whole selves without expectation.

What existed? Two individual separate people being their whole selves? Or a relationship? Did one replace the other? Did one become the solution to the other? Or did they appear and become possible because of each other? Distinct from one another but not separate. Growing from one to the other while being present with both.

Before us appeared a new possibility, for our individual selves and for our marriage. The feeling of it was so new, so different to anything we had had access to before, and yet we were still the same people. In fact, I was being more me than I'd ever been before, and so was he. We had not become bigger, better versions of ourselves; we were finally truly *being* ourselves. When I look back on the breakdown of our marriage, I recognized that somehow the picture of 'a relationship' and all the expectations that went with that – entangled in my story and survival, and his story and survival – had completely suffocated and blocked the freedom for each of us to be our whole, individual selves. As one took over from the other, it took the life, the love, the possibility out of both.

The same goes for you.

The moment you experience yourself in the space beyond your story – that moment of freedom, presence, truth, love, alignment – enjoy it, welcome it, be thankful for it. But the moment you want to use it to replace the story itself is the moment you also lose the freedom. When you can be with the story while also being in the space beyond the story, this allows you to be both space and human, freedom and human.

The aim was never for you to become another version of yourself. You were never meant to become a bigger, better, more lovable version of you. And why would you need to be this? Because you are and always have been already enough, and no one can be a richer, more alive expression of you than you. This is where you become more you than ever before. Less story, less strategy, less survival; more who you were born to be. When you can be with the story while simultaneously being with space beyond the story the frequency of who you are will be more in the here and now, in the present. And that's where life is. That's where love is. That's where everything alive is.

Next time you observe your story showing up, don't try to get rid of it; instead, learn to be with it. And as you are being with it, you will experience yourself simultaneously being in the space beyond the story, and that is where new possibilities will emerge.

This is the beginning of you creating new life born from a new space to stand, where you get to be the whole of who you were born to be.

EXERCISE: OBSERVING YOUR STORY

1. For a moment, observe the narrative moving through your mind, and any feelings moving through your body. Observe whether your story is present; whether the character you have known yourself to be is present.

2. Observe it and breathe, observe it and breathe, observe it and breathe.

3. Now notice yourself being the one observing. You may only get brief moments of experiencing this, when you're in the space observing while also being with the story present. Instead of trying to catch it or hold on to it, breathe even deeper and stay with this practice. Observe the story, while also observing yourself observing. The experience will flicker in and out, pockets of space flitting on and off like fireflies, but this is the beginning for you.

4. Once you have finished, describe in your journal how this practice was for you.

5. Look at your life and, choosing three examples, describe in your journal how different those three experiences would have been if you'd released yourself from trying to replace the experience with another, better one. What occurs if you open up to the possibility of allowing yourself to be with one experience while simultaneously opening yourself to something new?

6. Have there been times in your life when you've experienced these moments of freedom? One new possibility appearing from the presence of a past experience? Describe in your journal what was different in that moment. What allowed it to appear?

7. Are you ready now to fully surrender the fixing mindset and live in a new relationship with life in which there is a container for both shadow and light, story and space, human and spirit, love and freedom? Write in your journal what occurs for you around this inquiry and what you're letting go of to live in this way.

Curiosity and Wonder

When you first begin standing in a space beyond story, the experience can be so vast, unfamiliar and unknown that it's unsettling. After all this you'd imagine it to be the moment of nirvana, right? And it is, but it's simultaneously unsettling. Why? Well, imagine you're the frog (which you are), and after a lifetime of living in a well, you're sitting on the ledge at the top. Before you lies a huge, limitless space; below you is the well. You sit in this place, between both realities: the world of the story, which you are free to return to whenever you desire, and this expansive new space that is completely unknown.

I call this phase the newborn phase, because everyone I've ever worked with who arrives at this place has said the same thing: 'As I sit here in the space beyond my story – the story that is all I've ever known – I feel like a newborn baby learning from scratch how to live again, breathe again, walk again, be me again.' And it's the truth. You've spent your life surviving as who you thought you were within the story; and now, as you sit here with this complete space, you must learn to walk, breathe and live again from a new place of standing – a place aligned with your truth, your own heart, and your own authentic voice.

It's a tentative, vulnerable, sacred space to be in. It's so unknown that it may feel frightening and raw, so it's important to tread gently. Instead of being consumed with fear, this is where I like to invite you to call in curiosity and wonder. You're the butterfly that has just emerged from the chrysalis and now you need to allow your wings to unfurl. You've only known yourself as the caterpillar and now you're having to learn how to live and be in this new form. It's still you, and yet it's a new experience of you. It requires you to be patient, delicate, gentle, and slow with yourself; bringing curiosity instead of fear, bringing a sense of wonder instead of control. In this way you'll keep feeding this open spaciousness with a sense of limitless possibility.

A few months ago, I took my children out to the park. My son had just started learning to walk and it was so exciting for him. As we were slowly walking together towards the park, he wanted to stop to look and touch everything. And I let him. As I stood towering over this little boy, I watched him stop to look and touch a bush, pick up leaves that had fallen to the ground, and touch the leaves and branches on the bush. He touched a little stone that lay on the ground by his feet. As I watched him touch each thing with such curiosity and wonder, I noticed my mind getting noisy: *Why on Earth would he want to touch all these things?* And, as I heard this thought, I answered myself. *Because it is completely new and unknown to him and what comes with the new and unknown is an incredible possibility for discovery, wonder, magic.* I realized I'd walked past that bush a million times before and never stopped to look at it or touch its leaves. Why? Because I already 'know' what a bush is; I already 'know' what a leaf looks like and feels like. In my 'knowing', I don't bother to look, I don't bother to touch, I don't bother to discover. My knowing blocks me completely from allowing myself to discover this bush or stone in a new way.

As we began to walk again, we went past a rose bush. I observed myself look at the beautiful roses, ready to walk on past, my mind thinking: *I've smelt a rose before, it's just like all the other roses.* I was gobsmacked at how much life I may have blocked by this way of being. So instead I decided to take a 'leaf' (pun intended) out of my son's book and be curious to discover something new, something wondrous. I stood in front of the rose and began looking at it as if it were the very first time I'd ever seen such a magical thing as a rose. In an instant, it felt as though my eyes had opened up for the first time. Wow, this magical thing that is known as a rose is utterly remarkable!

I took in the petals, noticing how each one was perfectly independent of its neighbours, with barely noticeable differences only discernible if you really looked. I hadn't ever known that before. I noticed that my body responded to the way the flower opened up so fully, creating a feeling in my body and heart that felt wide and expansive. The intricacy of the pollen in the centre, with a bee drinking its nectar, was the most wondrous thing to witness. When I leaned down and pressed my whole nose into a flower to breathe in its incredible smell, it was honestly the most beautiful smell I'd ever known – delicate, sweet, alive. The whole experience standing there was like experiencing magic. The magic of life right there in front of me. The magic of discovery, curiosity, and wonder at the brand-new, unknown life appearing in the present.

Living in the story is living from the place of 'always already knowing'. When we're surviving in the character we already know how life goes. And we can no longer see the possibility of brand-new life appearing before us. You already 'know' yourself to be the one that is 'not enough', 'not worthy' or 'not safe', and therefore you can only see life through that lens. But living beyond the story offers a completely new space for you to live from. A completely new possibility that comes from every single moment appearing from the complete unknown.

Surrendering 'knowing' and being in the unknown can be deeply raw and exposing, and lead to feelings of vulnerability; simultaneously, it can be exceptionally alive and wondrous. The unknown offers the invitation to discover, to bring curiosity and wonder, and to truly see and listen and live with an awareness that wasn't available before.

Like my son exploring the bushes, like me exploring the rose, you must bring this curiosity and wonder into your life as you arrive at the newborn phase. Surrender the knowing, sit on the edge of the well, take in the vastness of space from this not knowing, and bring curiosity, bring wonder. Play, discover, allow new life – and new experience of who you are in it – to appear at the exact moment of looking. Take a moment here and really let this in.

- If you are not the one who is 'not enough', then who are you?

- If you are not the one who is 'not worthy' or 'not safe', then who are you?

- If you know that the parameters and possibilities and unfolding of your life no longer need to fit within the walls of the well, then what is possible?

- If you are not the characters in the story and the story is no longer what you know as your life, well then, what is?

The answer is: you don't know. Like a child looking ahead at their life with curiosity and wonder, welcome to the unknown! Play here, dance here, sing here, discover here.

Because here, in this space, anything is possible. Everything is possible.

And you can discover again and again and again. Discover who you are again, discover your heart again, discover your truth again. Discover your dreams again; choose from here.

Living from here, my love, is where you were born to live from, where there is limitless, endless possibility. Welcome home.

EXERCISE: BE CURIOUS

1. At least once this week, stop for a moment and really explore something in your space as if you are seeing it for the very first time. Maybe it's a flower or your partner's hands or your lover's lips or your own body. Describe in your journal what you learn and gain from this exercise.

2. Choose three examples of situations in your life when you were faced with the unknown and it brought up fear for you. Maybe it was the ending of a relationship, or the threshold of new behaviour, or right now at the thought of living beyond the story/survival? How did the fear impact on the situation? Did it get in the way? Did it block the flow? Did it shut you down? Did it cause you to go back into your story, or abandon yourself? Describe the impact for each example in your journal.

3. For each example in turn, imagine replacing fear with curiosity and wonder. Imagine looking ahead at the unknown and being filled with curiosity and wonder at what could possibly unfold. What could be possible for you if you were to bring curiosity and wonder to all areas of your life? Write a list of all the possibilities that would be there that weren't there before.

4. If you were to bring curiosity and wonder to every single threshold of the unknown ahead, how would this impact on your life? What does this change? What could you do differently? What actions would you take that you wouldn't have before? What dreams would you go for? What intimacy would you allow in? Play here in your journal as you allow yourself to describe the beauty of what is possible if fear is replaced by curiosity and wonder.

Unshakeable Trust

I have mentioned a few times about making the decision to trust, even if it seems impossible to do so. Now I want to expand more on this topic and explain why. Something happens the moment we make a decision to trust, or maybe something 'un-happens' (yes, I know that's not even a word, but often I find language can't always capture transformational awakening processes!): the grip we have on our story relaxes a little, our breathing may slow down, our being may ground more. Why? Because to choose to trust – even if it seems impossible – is a moment of surrender: a moment of letting go of survival and what we know; of surrendering to the unknown.

This kind of unshakeable trust is the anchor that will allow the expansion and unfurling of who you are as you move forwards from here. You stand now at the threshold of possibility, peering over the top of the well across the great unknown. This is the moment to make that choice to trust – not the blind-faith trust of the 'I give everything of myself to you' variety – but trust in this space beyond story: trust in the process of life and healing; trust in yourself and who you are beyond story. For if and when you manage to do that, you are actively stepping into a new unknown possibility. You are participating in the co-creation and rewriting of the unfolding for you from here. And, most significantly, you are doing it from standing in a different place: a place of trust over survival; a place of space over story; a place of presence over the past. You are looking at the vast unknown and saying *'Yes'* and opening to the new.

There are two types of trust. One is a childlike trust, when we put all our trust in outside sources – blindly, innocently, abandoning responsibility, laced with the hope of being rescued – yet the minute we detect any sign of imperfection, instability or error, we withdraw that trust immediately and go back into survival. This is how children trust, and it's how so many of us trust when we're living in the story.

The other kind of trust is a mature trust, when we do not put all our trust in someone or something 'out there'; instead, we choose to trust in who we are, beyond behaviour, beyond mistakes. We know outside circumstances change, people's behaviours change, and we mess up, but we choose to trust in who we are beyond this. To trust this way is to be wholly responsible for the unfolding of our life, fully committed to doing the best we can in each moment and, most importantly, completely aligned with living beyond the story and listening and responding beyond the story. This becomes the anchor we can trust we will return to; it's our human nature to always return here. And it is trustworthy.

When I look back at the first nine years of my marriage, I see clearly how much I operated from a place of childlike trust. I brought so much hope into the relationship, putting all my trust into the relationship like a child wanting Daddy to come take care of me. Then, if my husband let me down, behaved in a way that I found hurtful, or made mistakes, I'd chalk it up as evidence that I should immediately withdraw my trust and end the relationship.

He did the same with me, leaving us both in a continuous cycle of survival, withdrawal and self-protecting, with no deeper trust available. Nothing can thrive in such a space except more survival. That's why I felt the need to be such a warrior woman all the time – ready to fight and win battles, ready to protect myself. Deep down, I didn't fully trust who I was without all that protection and I didn't trust life to support me if I ever surrendered it. I'd still been the terrified little four-year-old that felt unsafe, but I'd hidden myself inside an armour casing of strong, assertive, grown-up woman.

As my husband and I started experiencing this new profoundly beautiful love, I found my heart opening full and wide to him in a way it never had before. One day, however, he was cranky and got snappy and a bit shitty, and I noticed how quickly I shut my heart and withdrew – how quickly that became my evidence that I should leap back into the story. As I went for a walk to reflect on what was going on for me, I realized how conditional my relationship to trust remained – that four-year-old was still looking for evidence that she had to do it alone to be safe in survival. I'd been basing my trust on what I achieved, how I behaved and whether I got things right or not. Basing my trust on actions – on behaviour, personality, and opinions – was always going to be so unreliable and conditional, however. It meant I'd always be let down somehow – I'd always find the evidence to stay in survival. Having this type of relationship with trust was part of the story itself; it was part of the survival. If I truly wanted to live beyond this, it would require me to take a risk – a risk to trust in who I am rather than what I do, to trust in life and my relationship with it. This was the first step for me: I had to make the choice to first trust in myself before I could ever feel safe enough to trust in another – and to trust my husband.

I took a little time to look much deeper at myself.

Trust in Who You Are

I've made mistakes – some big ones – and I'll probably make more (hopefully not such big ones, but you never know!). Through it all – through my childhood, the addiction, the pain I've carried within myself – I've never given up. No matter what, I've always found ways to keep moving through. I've continued to find ways to create life and to heal; or, more likely, I've allowed life and healing to find me.

Trusting in who you are beyond

the story is not trusting blindly;

it's consciously choosing to trust

who you are and to stand by that

choice every moment of every day.

~

I've always been open to learning, listening and surrendering. The essence of who I am is still this way. As I allowed this to land within me, I began to see myself for who I really am.

At the core I saw a person I could trust. I accepted I would make mistakes, but I trust that, when in the midst of these experiences, who I am will know the right thing to do and the right way to go. Being human means we are just that: human. We will always have a mind and we will always have a story. We are imperfect, we make mistakes; our minds will try to pull us back into survival, because that is the nature of the mind. As long as we are human, we will experience fear and pain and vulnerability, and this may be uncomfortable.

But beyond all the human-ness you're a being – one that's not defined by all those things we do and feel and think. Beyond all such things you are a being; beyond the story is not a character, there's no need to survive, because you're already whole. This essence of who you are is one that can be trusted, and the moment you can make this choice for yourself, and then commit to standing by this choice, is the moment the doors will begin to open – those doors that had slammed shut in an attempt to protect and survive. First they'll open to you, and then to life itself.

Take a moment to look at yourself. Go much deeper here and allow yourself to tap into the essence of who you truly are – beyond mistakes, beyond behaviour, without judgement – bringing only compassion and inquiry. Let yourself see yourself here. Can you see the essence of your being, which has been trying to solve a problem, trying to find a way home. Can you connect to the essence of your being, which has been doing the best it can with the awareness and information you had at the time?

This is your truth. This is your true essence. This is who you are. This is who I want you to see when you see yourself. Don't define yourself by what you've done or haven't done, but by the alive, vulnerable, raw being within – the one who's been doing its best all this time.

In doing so, you can make the decision to trust in who you are rather than what you do. It's your choice to make: to let yourself off the hook once and for all; to finally begin seeing yourself the way you've longed to be seen by the world, by your parents, by society, by life. This is your invitation to make the decision to trust in who you are beyond the story. It's not trusting blindly, but consciously choosing to take the risk to trust in this being that you are, and to stand by this every moment of every day.

This is the gateway to a greater love far beyond what is available or possible within the realms of the story and survival.

Once I finally made the conscious choice to trust myself beyond the story, something significant shifted within me: a safety, a solidity, a strength arrived – something grounding, still, peaceful.

When I returned from that walk, I sat with my husband, looked him straight in the eyes, and shared what I'd discovered about myself and my relationship to trust. As we looked into each other's eyes, I began to see him differently. As I was coming from a place of trust in myself, it was safe to open my heart to this human being that had shown himself so vulnerably to me. Even though I could never control his behaviour or thoughts or feelings, and even though love offers no guarantees, what I could do was show up for myself to the best of my ability. He too had made mistakes and he was going to make more. And yet, he was still here with me; showing up, doing the work, doing his best.

Despite everything he has lived through in this life – all the pain he has carried – he was still here.

There and then, as I looked into his eyes, I made the decision to love this man for who he is beyond the story. And the trust I had in myself allowed me to love him more fully than ever before.

It felt so vulnerable, exposing, raw and scary. There is simply no way of knowing whether I'll get hurt again or whether I'll be abandoned or whether it'll work out – all the fears that had kept me in my story for so long. But the trust in myself will always be there to guide me each moment. There and then, I made a stand for something greater than surviving. I made a stand for life and for love. My husband looked me straight in the eyes and made the same choice. In that moment, we made the decision to be a space for something greater than our stories and protecting our hearts and creating pictures and keeping safe and surviving. In that moment, it was as though an anchor was dropped, mooring us to the foundations of what was possible beyond story.

Six months after our marriage had died, six months after he'd moved out of the family home and we'd separated, my husband and I created a new love; a new bonding. We renewed our vows to each other on the most incredible beach in New Zealand, witnessed only by our two children and two relatives. It felt as though a completely new possibility had been born for us both. Not because either of us had saved the other or fulfilled the other's emptiness, but because – for the first time for us both – all of who we are was welcomed and had been seen and shared and witnessed and chosen. We'd seen the worst of each other and the best, and we were committed to showing up for the greater good.

At the core of it was an anchoring steeped in trust: trust in the being beyond story; trust in life beyond survival; trust in the space beyond the knowing. Trust. From this trust anything can grow with freedom. Freedom to be human, imperfect, not knowing, raw, vulnerable, afraid. Freedom to be both the story and beyond the story. The trust I gave myself allowed me to unfurl into my full, whole self. The trust he gave himself enabled him to unfurl into his full, whole self. The trust we created for each other allowed a new possibility for partnership and marriage to be birthed.

As we read our new vows to each other, I looked over at him and realized I'd never known love this way before. I am more me than I'd ever experienced and he was more him. An absolute freedom and holding of our two whole, individual selves while simultaneously bonded through an unshakeable trust that had formed between us. For the first time in my 40 years on this Earth, I discovered what it felt like to love and be loved with complete freedom.

Becoming Fully Anchored

This journey is not about finding romance, or finding the perfect love story. To even want that already feeds into survival to compensate for something else. This is about living and loving from a place of wholeness as all of who you truly are. The love that has grown between my husband and me is not as a result of finding the answer to anything. It's not because we fixed anything. It's because I'm committed to living from the place beyond my story and so is he.

From this place there's no need to fill the other's emptiness, or fix the other's pain, or live in the other's pictures or expectations. From here we're committed to living and being our authentic, whole selves – in our individual lives and in our marriage.

Living from this place allows you to remember something that's always been there: that you never needed to change anything or fix anything in order to 'find love', because from this place beyond the story, you are love. You are whole, you are enough and there is nothing to be fixed. From this place love is limitlessly possible.

In your life, you'll encounter situations and people who, even when you can see deep within their true essence, are just not willing nor ready to do the work to be accountable for themselves. When that happens, trust yourself even more to know whether this is where you want to be giving of your heart. When you can draw on this deeper trust within you, you'll forever have a source of wisdom to draw from – the wisdom of your own deep knowing, stemming from a foundation of trust in yourself.

Who you are is so much greater than stories and beliefs and behaviours and patterns.

Who you are is limitless.

Make the choice to trust this so you can truly live and love with freedom.

EXERCISE: TRUST

1. In your journal, describe your relationship with trust up to this point. Have you been operating from a place of childlike trust or mature trust?

2. Give 3–5 examples of situations in your life when childlike trust has kept you in the story and blocked the flow of your life and the full expression of yourself. Write in detail how it impacted on you, on others, and on your behaviour

3. Take a moment to scan through your life and list all the times when you have shown up against all odds, turned things around, shown courage, been brave, surprised yourself. And even when you've made mistakes, what was really there underneath the behaviour? Try to see the need and pain, bringing compassion.

4. List all the reasons why you could begin to trust who you are rather than what you have done or how you have behaved.

5. List all the qualities that make you *you*. For example: *I am sensitive, strong, kind. I am brave, courageous, honest.* Write as long a list as you can and then read it aloud to yourself, pausing after each quality to let it land and let yourself receive it. Let it in.

6. If you are ready now to commit to trusting who you are within a framework of mature trust, write a letter to the child within you, acknowledging all that child's needs and the behaviours, mistakes or breakdowns that those needs led to – behaviours you've been holding on to as 'evidence' of your untrustworthiness. Acknowledge the root of the behaviour; bring your compassion, seeing, and awareness to each moment. Describe how you can see you've always been trying to solve a problem, but no one taught you another way. And how you are ready now to learn new ways.

7. Finish off by making a committed decision to trust in who you are, and to hold this space as the mature adult you are today.

INFINITY MEDITATION

Close your eyes, and take a deep breath in, allowing the breath to touch the insides of your whole being, feeding and nurturing you, nourishing you with life. Expand your lungs and fill them up. And as you exhale, just let go.

Take another breath in, drawing it up into your abdomen; creating spaciousness, nourishing and feeding the insides of your being, receiving life. Again, as you exhale, just let go.

Once again, breathe in – a deep, slow breath that feeds your body with life force, creating spaciousness all the way up to your heart and expanding your lungs. As you exhale, just let go.

Continue to allow your body to breathe in this way as you bring your awareness inwards.

I invite you now to become present to the story, to the well that you've been in. See it with your mind's eye, allow it to be entirely present before you. Recognize it, become familiar with it, know it fully. And then allow the image in your mind's eye to dissolve completely before you – utterly dissolved, gone. Surrender.

Now bring forth all the views and opinions that you've held: what is 'beauty', what is 'worth', what is 'safe', what is 'love'. Allow all the views and opinions that you've absorbed and learned to come to the fore. And now let them dissolve completely – gone. Surrender.

Next, bring forth all the pictures you have in your mind of what you need to be happy – all that you've been striving for. See every detail of them; know them fully. And then allow them to dissolve completely – gone. Surrender.

Now bring forth all your connections to culture: the culture you have been brought up in, the culture in your family's line, all culture that exists on this planet. Bring it forth, see it all, then let it dissolve completely – gone. Surrender.

Now bring forth all the ideas and opinions and views of what is man and what is woman, of what a woman's body should look like, of what a woman should look like and be like, of what a man's body should look like, and what a man should be like or look like. See it, let it be present fully for you. And now let it dissolve completely – gone. Surrender.

Bring forth all the ideas and views you have of skin colour. See it, let it be present fully for you. Now let it dissolve completely. Surrender.

Now bring forth all ideas and views of love and worth, and let them dissolve completely. Surrender.

Now bring forth all language. See it, let it be fully present, and let it dissolve completely – gone. Surrender, breathing into this complete space, this spaciousness. Surrender to space: space that you are, space that you're in, space all around you. Spaciousness.

Allow your next in-breath to expand the space that you are so that you expand to fill the entire room.

On your next in-breath, allow the space that you are to expand to fill the whole street.

On your next in-breath, allow the space that you are to expand to fill the entire country.

On your next in-breath allow the space that you are to expand to fill the entire planet.

Finally, on your next in-breath, allow the space that you are to expand to fill infinity. Breathe. Simply be here. You are not in a life; you are a life. You are everything and you are nothing.

Continue to be here in this spaciousness for a minimum of 10 minutes. Listen from this space of stillness. This is who you are.

When you are ready, allow your awareness to return to the present moment. Regulate your breath. Wiggle your toes and your fingers. Let your body stretch and move in whatever way it needs. Then very, very gently, slowly open your eyes.

Use your journal to write down any insights, seeings or learnings you gained from this practice. This is a powerful meditation you can use regularly to connect to the expansiveness of who you are.

CHAPTER 8
The End of the Beginning

*'Nothing ever goes away until it has
taught us what we need to know.'*

PEMA CHÖDRÖN

At the core of human existence is a beating human heart. But what is the heart? What is its purpose? On a physical level, it is the organ that literally pumps life through our body, continuously, autonomously, whether we acknowledge it or are aware of it or are connected to it in any way. On a deeper level, the heart is known in Eastern philosophies as the House of Shen: the home in which all truth and answers lie; the seat of consciousness and truth; the place to come and listen for guidance and truth. There are no stories in the heart, there's no language, there are no beliefs or pictures, there's no fear. The heart is the space of stillness behind the words, behind the story.

And the heart is where the whole story and survival begin too.

The moment our story is created, when we begin identifying with the conditioning in the mind, is a moment of pain or threat to the heart –

a moment of heartbreak, vulnerability and love. In this moment, we disconnect from our true self: we begin surviving, led by the mind, and we depart our heart – the home of our truth. Our authentic truth. Your authentic truth. While living in the story we can and will create lives aligned only with the story, and we end up creating and living lives that just don't align with who we are. We end up in jobs that fit the pictures others have sold to us as representative of who we're 'supposed' to be. We mould ourselves into characters we're told we are and who we tell ourselves we need to be. All are attempts to be loved and accepted by the world, but none have anything to do with listening and honouring the authentic truth of our hearts.

And so here we are, in the final chapter of this book, and it is time to return home – the home of your heart.

Become Who You Truly Are

The greatest, most generous act that any of us can do for ourselves, for our loved ones and for this planet, is to become who we truly are. This is not only a dream for you to fulfil, it is life's dream for you too. When you are living in alignment with your true whole self, you're an authentic space through which life can be expressed. You're a vibrational frequency of wholeness and flow, energy and power. Your energy becomes more alive, your health begins to thrive, and your mental and emotional wellbeing can thrive. Alignment is the best medicine there is for everyone, because it is led by authenticity rather than trauma.

When we come from our wholeness (rather than the story), we bring wholeness to life and to all of those around us. By raising the frequency, we bring healing to the spaces and places that are in survival, that are in separation, that are stuck in the story. It was our core desire for love that first caused us to disconnect, and it is a core desire for love that will bring us home. To listen to the whispers of your heart is an act of love. To do the work you have done in this book is an act of love. To allow yourself to feel and be with what's there is an act of love. And to allow yourself to dream again is an act of love.

There's a much greater purpose to your life here and only when you're beyond the story can you begin listening to what that might be. That's when you can begin to own that your presence here actually matters, your existence here actually matters, how you use this life actually matters. In fact, it matters greatly. You have done surviving and it got you so far – and let's not pretend it wasn't useful; let's not pretend it didn't serve you in many ways. It did; it served its purpose. Now that you've seen over the top of the well, however, and seen the stone walls, and hopefully even had a glimpse of who you authentically are, surviving is not your purpose here and it never was. Now is the time to choose thriving: to choose blooming; to choose your full, unlimited and complete unfurling into who you were always born to be – returning home to the one you were before the heartbreak, before the split, before the disconnect. To your authentic self.

All the life experiences, struggles, challenges and surviving have been of undeniable value, however. They are what has matured you and offered you an even richer foundation for the birthing of your life from here.

This life will not last forever – we all so easily forget this. There'll be a time when you'll reach the end. When that time comes, how do you want to feel when you look back on how you've lived your life? How have you used this life? How have you showed up? Yes, this applies to me too. I want to know that I've truly lived and that I made it count – and not just for me, but for all those around me, and for life itself.

I want to know that I have served life well.

Here, in the space beyond the story, you no longer need to be defined by the past and you no longer need be led by fear. Instead, you are faced with the limitless possibility of what can be created and lived beyond this. What is it that you dream of? What lies within your heart that is whispering to you, longing for your attention? What moves you so deeply that it fills your whole body with meaning and purpose? Beyond the layers that create our differences – beyond language, beyond skin colour, beyond culture and heritage, beyond class, beyond all the things that create our difference – we as a species are so similar.

Those differences we do have, however, are important and should not be dismissed. In fact, they should be owned, honoured, loved and welcomed. In doing so we can use them to create and weave the fabric of our life's unfolding from here. Let life be a blank canvas and let every moment we've lived – every experience we've had, every aspect of who we are – be the paint and colours that make the art possible. To allow our true, authentic voice to be fully expressed in this world is the phase of birthing – rewriting a new story for ourselves, not as a bigger, better version of ourselves, but by actually being our true self.

In the exact moments of allowing the old story to dissolve we are birthing a new one. Every single time we take the risk of listening to our heart and letting it lead our life – every time we take the risk of expressing our true voice, every time we take an action aligned with who we truly are – we create more of our life from this authentic place to stand, allowing ourselves to thrive and unfurl even more into our truest self.

Let Your Heart Lead the Way

This is a new way to be; a dance with life where we are equal co-creators, actively participating in our own authentic maturation while bringing this frequency to life itself. Life is a master teacher, you see. There are really no accidents and there are no right or wrong turns (nor have there ever been). In this new dance with life, every single moment of our life can become useful if we're willing to let our hearts lead the way.

When I look back on my life, this is crystal clear. Every single thing I've lived and experienced has become useful somehow to who I am and how I live today. In no longer trying to survive it and resist it, I can actually begin to use it in valuable and purposeful ways. By taking the risk of listening to my heart, I heard how much I care about helping other people heal, and how much I care about connection, intimacy, awakening, freedom. Why? Partly because it's what I needed myself, to grow and heal; and partly because it's just part of who I authentically am. The past feeds the future, the future inspires the past, and the present is where all of it can be created, because we are now able to hold it all in a place of awareness and wholeness. Life is an ever-flowing exchange – death becomes a birth; birth becomes a death. When we live from this space of the heart, when we live in honour of what we have lived and who we authentically are, when we live beyond the story, we become co-creators in this ever-changing flow.

When there are no more pictures to try to fit ourselves into, and there is no longer an attachment to the programming of our minds stemming from the past, all there is left is our truth. That truth is the most authentic gift we can ever give and use and draw from.

So, my dear, let's look at you. In the final invitation of surrender. A surrendering of what's left of who you thought you were and needed to be that's getting in the way of who you were born to be, that's getting in the way of life's dream for you.

Close your eyes and connect to your heart – beyond the mind, beyond the noise, beyond the story. Surrender all that is left and ask yourself these important questions.

- Who are you now?

- What do you love?

- What moves you at the deepest level?

- What dreams lie in your heart that you have not yet dared say out loud?

- What brings you joy?

- What bring you life?

- What do you care about?

- What do you want to feel and see when you're at the end of this sacred gift of life and you look back on how you lived it?

Let these questions land deeply into the rawness of your sacred, vulnerable heart. You don't need to have the answers straight away. In fact, you don't need to have any answers right now. Instead, all that's needed now is for you to allow yourself to ask the questions and for you to let the questions themselves lead you from here.

Let your heart lead you, let life lead you, let your listening and awareness lead you.

You have a mind; use it, but do not become your mind.

Speak all that lies within your heart now, own it so you can begin living it.

And then begin to dream, dream it all. And because this one life is all you get, dream big.

EXERCISE: INSPIRATION

1. Describe in your journal an occasion in your life when something moved you so deeply that it inspired you more than anything else. What was it about this experience that moved you so much? Please list 3–4 of the qualities of this moment that moved you so deeply.

2. Close your eyes and take three deep breaths in. Now be in that moment when you were so moved. Feel those feelings of the qualities that moved you so much. Let it fill you up entirely. Note in your journal what it felt like and what came for you in this exercise. These are the qualities that matter to you in your life.

3. Now, as you stand here beyond the story, where anything is

possible, where you have learned what moves you and means so much to you, what is your vision, what is your dream? Whatever it is, let it be big. Let it be so big it makes your stomach flip to even say it aloud.

4. Close your eyes and visualize yourself being the person in that vision. Let it fill your entire being with how it feels. Just be in it, breathing and luxuriating in it for a while.

5. When you open your eyes, describe in your journal what came from this for you.

6. Write down what actions you are willing to take to bring your vision into reality.

Conclusion

*'Do not grow old, no matter how long you live.
Never cease to stand like curious children before
the Great Mystery into which we were born.'*

ALBERT EINSTEIN

I want to admit something to you. For many of the years I dedicated to my path of healing, I was motivated solely for myself, my own longing – driven by my deep desire to become free of the suffering and struggle and suppression and prison I was confined in, within the story of my past. Then, a few years ago, a significant moment occurred for me.

It was a typical morning, albeit with a level of peace and compassion in my heart that just wouldn't have been possible before. As I was drinking my morning coffee, I had another big moment of awakening. All those years of longing to be free; all the blood, sweat and tears I'd shed in workshop rooms and therapy sessions; all the books I'd read and journals I'd written in; all the moments of surrender and courage it had taken to face it all and feel it all, because the calling within me to become free was so undeniable I couldn't *not* keep going – it had all led me here to this moment. Here I was – sitting in this peace, finally able to reap the gifts of all those years – when I realized: *My God, this was never all about me. It was never meant to just be about me. It can't just be about me.*

The pain I've carried and have healed and continue to heal, my mother carried before me, and my grandmother before her, and her grandmother too. And my father, and his father, and his father before him. My pain is your pain; my suffering is your suffering. We are not separate entities here on this Earth. What we've carried has not just happened randomly. It's all been part of the sequence of life that has gone before us and life around us and after us. We're all an extension of each other. When one of us finds the courage to keep following this calling to heal, it helps us all break free of the confines of the stories, the conditioning, the survival. It helps us all to face the past and be with it fully right here in this present, in service of bringing wholeness to what we carry that is in separation.

We heal for each other.

This is the sacred truth we have forgotten.

We are all one species and we are all alive beings, integrated into the fabric of life itself. Every moment of trauma we've received and inherited, we turn on ourselves, creating more separation that we then act out into the world. The sequence is endless and will continue to be endless unless we're willing to participate in creating change.

And that change begins with you. Like your journey at the beginning of this book, we as a species are on the cusp of an ending on a collective scale. The ending of the old paradigm; the endless sequence of separation and trauma that have created the fundamental structures and systems of how we've been living. But we haven't been living; we've been surviving – led by fear, led by unhealed trauma, creating more of the same. Fear creating more fear, hate creating more hate, blame creating more blame. In our survival, we've forgotten that we're part of the whole, we're part of the Earth, we're part of the animal kingdom, we're part of the natural world and we're all an expression of life. Survival cannot create life; it can only create more survival.

Consider the problems we face now on our planet: the issues around climate, land and seas, and the extinction of animals; the many suffering from hunger, poverty, and homelessness; the utterly unequal distribution of wealth and privilege and sovereignty; the oppression and racism and separation. Every one of these major issues is a direct consequence of human beings leading from a place of fear and separation, stuck in survival, confined within the story. This blinds us from seeing more clearly, but we are not our trauma, we are not our stories. We are not separate. Who we are is wholeness; who we are is life. Everything is alive, and we cannot create change on our planet by coming from the same place that caused the problems in the first place.

So, I want to bring this back to you for one final time in our journey together through this book.

You are not merely just one amongst billions on this planet. You are an integral, fundamental part of the whole. Please do not think that who you are being in this world is too small to make a difference. In fact, who you are being makes the world of difference: to your children, your partners, your friends, to the man at the bus stop or the woman on the corner. You are a thread in the sequence to which and through which we are all connected.

Every time one of us does the work to make whole all the aspects within ourselves that are creating more separation on this planet, it allows the vibrational force from that person to shift and expand. It raises awareness; raises consciousness. It expands our capacity to be love, to be compassion, to be whole. We embody more power, more life, more purpose, more clarity, more seeing. Our connection to life deepens; our connection to the earth, the plants, the sky, the trees, to each other and to everything on this planet deepens.

Every time one of us shifts in consciousness, we participate in shifting the consciousness amongst our species. Just as you are allowing the old character to die as you birth a new story of your life, we together participate in allowing the old paradigm to die as we open up the space for the birthing of a new one.

This is you.

This is why you are here now.

This is why you were called to pick up this book.

Every time you heal, you change the vibrational field in which you stand and live from. You are impacting both the past and the future. And that is the bigger picture.

When I look at my family today – my sisters, my brothers, my mother, my husband, my children – everyone has been affected by this work. Every moment I become more aligned with my own wholeness and authenticity, a little more wholeness and healing moves through my family line. You see, this was never ever about feeling better, this was about maturation, this was about our evolution. Maturation is not a process of finding or adding more; it is a process of surrendering.

Surrendering all that we are not, all that is not aligned, all that is not authentic, in order for what is true, what is authentic, and what is whole to birth through.

Here's a secret: you may have thought you picked up this book in order to fix your problems. Really, however, life tapped you on the shoulder, inviting you to surrender who you thought you were, so you can remember who you are.

You are being called to participate in a global shift of humanity, so hold this bigger picture in your heart today and every day. Hold it when pain comes again and you have to be uncomfortable. Hold it when you're back in the well and you have to remember how to get yourself out once again. Hold it when life is challenging and hard and you need to invoke that courageous stand that has been within you all along. Hold it as a solid, unshakeable commitment deep within your heart to coming home and waking up and becoming free.

Because this is what love is: to show up this way, with this much courage, with this much commitment, with this much power.

This is love. And love is what is needed today.

You started this book at the beginning of the end. If you have been paying attention, then you are now at the end of a process that will allow you to truly begin. You can now turn the final pages and continue this process into your life. Please take these words and live them; integrate them into every part of who you're being and how you live. Let them transform from words of truth on a page into your own lived, integrated truth for yourself and your life.

This is what you came here for. You were never someone who needed to be fixed, because you were never broken. You were never someone who needed to find yourself, because who you are has always been here. And you never needed to get a life, because you are life. There is only one more thing left to do now, and that is to go and live, and to live fully and wholly aligned with your heart and truth.

So thank you for picking up this book. Thank you for answering the call. Thank you for reading this all the way to these last words. Thank you. I see you; I see how brave you are and how much love you bring here. I'm here with you too, and every step of the way I walk with you. Together we surrender, in our imperfect, messy, clunky way, to answer the call. And to bring us home.

Sometimes we have to row

far from the shore in order

to reach new lands.

~

Resources

Training and Schools

The International School of Macrobiotics, Murtwell House, Diptford, Totnes TQ9 7NQ, United Kingdom (macroschool.co.uk)

The Concord Institute for Integral Studies, Unit 2, 2–4 Thane Works, London N7 7NU, United Kingdom (concordinstitute.com)

The Alchemy of Breath (alchemyofbreath.com)

The Alchemy of Being: Academy of Maturation Coaching (nickyclinch.com)

Books

The Self-Healing Cookbook, Kristina Turner (Earthtones Press, first published 1988, latest edition 2012)

The Power of Now, Eckart Tolle (Namaste Publishing, first edition 1997; Yellow Kite, latest edition 2020)

The End of Your World, Adyashanti (Sounds True Inc, 2009)

The More Beautiful World Our Hearts Know is Possible, Charles Eisenstein (North Atlantic Books, 2013)

When Things Fall Apart, Pema Chödrön (Shambhala, latest edition 2016)

Comfortable with Uncertainty, Pema Chödrön (Shambhala, 2008)

Descartes' Error, Antonio R. Damasio (Grosset Putnam, 1994, latest edition 2006)

Be Here Now, Ram Dass (Crown Publications, 1971)

Plant Medicine Retreat Centres

The Temple of the Way of Light (templeofthewayoflight.org)

Ron Wheelock (elpurguero.com)

Further resources

All meditations, breathwork practices, bodywork practices and much more are available at nickyclinch.com

Acknowledgements

It has been an extremely moving experience to reflect on how many people in my life have had an impact on this book being born, and for me to become the woman I needed to become in order to write it. Even though I may have been the one who put my fingers to the keyboard and wrote down the text, this book was written through a collaboration of courageous hearts, human lives, teachers, mentors, friends and family members – all of whom have moved me, taught me, and changed me in their own beautiful ways. I will name some here, but know that this list is merely the visible trunk of the oak tree we get to see and adore in its magnificence. Hidden beneath the surface, however, are hundreds of roots. These roots are the people who may not be named here but have played an integral part in the creation of the whole.

Firstly, I'd like to acknowledge my darling husband Kevin, who has walked beside me through the rough and the smooth. Who showed up and did the work with me, lived the process with me and committed to something greater than we could feel but not yet see. Without him, I could not have lived the beauty of what I lived through in order to share these words with you in this book. On a practical level, writing this book through a global pandemic and global lockdowns was beyond challenging, and my husband simply continued to hold space for our babies, our home and me so that I could complete my work here. Without him these words would not have landed on these pages.

I want to acknowledge my mother, father and siblings, and my incredible friends, all of whom have supported me endlessly, no matter what. My editor Michelle Pilley, who trusted me and life enough to let the original book idea go because I knew that it was this book that was meant to be born at this moment in time. My incredible book team: Emily Arbis, Valeria Huerta, Kate Lane, Hannah Bryce, Suzy Ashworth and Nikki Van De Car. My teacher and mentor David Norris, who once told me he would never give me words to use; instead he would speak them to me only, to allow me to absorb them deeply into my pores so I can then speak them, share them and express them through my own voice and heart. I am forever grateful and humbled to have such a teacher in my life.

To my beautiful children, who give me a reason every day to get up and dig deeper into my own soul so I may continue to participate in carving out a better world for them somehow.

To my clients who come to me with such courage, such heart; please know that holding space for you and witnessing your healing and maturation is a great honour and privilege that changes me every day and gives me enormous fulfilment and purpose.

To the near-strangers who shower me with generosity and encouragement every day through my community. And lastly, but certainly not least, to Emma Cannon, my soul sister, my navigation buddy. For the endless moments in time you have inspired me, listened to me and walked this path of healing and growth with me through the joy and through immensely challenging times. You are my anchor, you are my wings, you are my heart.

ABOUT THE AUTHOR

Nicky Clinch is a Maturation Coach, an Integrative Holistic Counsellor, a Conscious Connected Breathwork facilitator and an author. She mentors people from all over the world, leads sell-out life-changing retreats and facilitates the gateway maturation programme, 'Listening to Life'. Founder and head facilitator of The Alchemy of Being: The Academy of Maturation Coaching, she trains people around the world to become powerful certified maturation facilitators and containers for human beings to come home to being.

Nicky is also the founder and host of the Soul Surgery Podcast, which focuses on sharing fundamentally important conversations for creating a new paradigm for humanity. Episodes have featured prominent voices in their fields, such as Dr Jaiya John, Dr Gabor Mate, Dr David Norris and Michaela Boehm.

Rapidly becoming a leading figure and teacher in the field of transformation and healing, Nicky has spoken at events across the globe and featured in *Vogue, Red, Grazia, Metro, The Telegraph, The Times, Psychologies, Natural Health* and many more.

f nickyclinchempowerment

◎ @nicky_clinch

🐦 @NickyClinch

You Tube Nicky Clinch

www.nickyclinch.com

HAY HOUSE

Look within

Join the conversation about latest products, events, exclusive offers and more.

 Hay House

 @HayHouseUK

 @hayhouseuk

 healyourlife.com

We'd love to hear from you!